MW01516736

THRIVING
Relationships

*A Couples' Guide to
Relational Transformation*

DR DAMILOLA ADINGUPU, PHD
MR IFECHUKWUDE ADINGUPU

◆ FriesenPress

One Printers Way
Altona, MB R0G 0B0
Canada

www.friesenpress.com

Copyright © 2023 by ATKA Solutions Incorporated
First Edition — 2023

Photographer: James Idowu

All rights reserved. No part of this couple's guide may be reproduced or transmitted in any form or by any means, electronic or mechanical, including photocopy, recording, or any information storage or retrieval system without permission in writing from the copyright holder or agent clearly identified, except in the case of brief quotations embodied in critical articles or reviews.

No part of this publication may be reproduced in any form, or by any means, electronic or mechanical, including photocopying, recording, or any information browsing, storage, or retrieval system, without permission in writing from FriesenPress.

ISBN
978-1-03-918984-3 (Hardcover)
978-1-03-918983-6 (Paperback)
978-1-03-918985-0 (eBook)

1. FAMILY & RELATIONSHIPS, MARRIAGE

Distributed to the trade by The Ingram Book Company

This couples' guide belongs to:

....

....

....

Table of Contents

Acknowledgments

We are grateful to the couples who participated in the beta reading of this book and gave us valuable feedback that ultimately made this book better than we could have made it on our own. These couples not only gave us their time, but they were also willing to be vulnerable and engage in the activities with the courage to face relevant issues in their relationships.

To our children, Arinzechukwu, Tobenna, and Kenechi, we are so grateful that you all are willing to share your parents with our world and cheer us on this journey. Thank you for your curiosity at such young ages and for asking us often why we're doing "TheMarriageAdvocates." This has helped us to keep our "why" focused. To our extended family, we are grateful for our experiences with you that shaped us and for your support and prayers.

To the community that served as our backup singers within the first three years of our marriage and mentored us to develop a healthy marriage, Rediscover, Exeter, UK: we are grateful for your investment of love in our lives. Your impact on our marriage within the first three years set us on a trajectory that put us on the path we're following now.

The professional team at FriesenPress has been highly supportive and helpful, and we are grateful.

Introduction

A healthy connection to others, especially our partners, is vital to our happiness and well-being. The quality of our relationships greatly impacts our mental, emotional, and physical health. How can we have healthy relationships, especially when many of us come from backgrounds that didn't equip us with the skills and habits to develop such relationships?

There is good news. Habits and skills that foster healthy relationships can be learned. We all have a wonderful ability to learn how to connect with our partners securely, communicate respectfully and lovingly, manage conflict, and develop many other skills that will enhance the development of a healthy relationship. This book is a guide, informed by research, that will take you on a journey from a broken background to a thriving relationship.

This journey will involve you acknowledging any brokenness you may have experienced in your past, facing it head-on, and saying to yourself and perhaps someone you trust, "That experience had an impact on me." This is an important step because avoiding your experiences' reality has inherent consequences you can't avoid.

After acknowledgment must come the conscious awareness of the areas in your life and relationship where the impact of those experiences may be positive or negative. Acknowledging and becoming aware alone doesn't result in a transformed relationship. The crucial third step is to act in ways that will support healthy growth in yourself and your relationship past that place of brokenness.

This couples' guide will help you acknowledge experiences in your past that are impacting your relationship, give you tools to become more aware of how these experiences may be playing out in your relationship, and support you with activities you can engage in to help you build a thriving relationship. You'll have opportunities to learn about yourself, each other, and your relationship dynamic, whilst getting equipped with tools to grow a healthy marriage.

CHAPTER 1

Remembering

HOW YOU STARTED
AND
WHERE YOU WANT TO BE

Every relationship has a story of how it began. You probably have a beautiful or unusual story of how you met, with memories from your dating period that are sweet and romantic. Over time in your relationship, you might have forgotten how you started and the reasons you chose each other in the first place.

We have an unusual story of how we met. We met on a train journey. Ife was on his way to work, and Dami was on her way to college. Dami was settled in a carriage, studying for an exam by using cue cards, when Ife walked down the carriage and asked to sit next to Dami. She said yes, and, well, that was the end of studying on that trip. There was nonstop laughter the entire journey. We both remember that day fondly, and we still giggle at the events that unfolded in the short time we spent together.

Reminiscing about beautiful memories is easy when we have positive feedback from our partner, and everything is going well. But when our relationship is in a difficult place, if we don't train our minds to remember the good, it will focus on and amplify the bad. Our brain seems to have a natural tendency to be more attentive to negative experiences, the so-called negativity bias. [1]

It's important to acknowledge the areas in which you may have focused on the negative experiences and been blinded to the good ones. Accept that this may have contributed to a negative trajectory in your relationship. To break this negativity bias, you must act and make a conscious, consistent effort to bring to your mind the good things about your partner and your relationship.

Activity 1 (10 minutes)

Do this together.

Share your memories of the first time you met one another.

What attracted you to each other?

"It takes one thought, one second, one moment, or positive memory to act as a catalyst for the light to gradually seep in again."
—Fearne Cotton

Balancing and Alignment: A Unit within a Supporting Community

When you get married, you become a unit that's supposed to flourish within the context of a nourishing community. Many couples, however, become an isolated unit after getting married. This may be because of cultural or religious teachings. Some individuals were taught that once you get married, all you have and need is each other, and whatever happens in the home should be resolved in the home. This, coupled with the fact that life traumas and experiences haven't prepared many individuals to be good partners (even though they're probably good people), can cause the marriage to quickly descend into a state of chaos.

Think of a classic car that was built from materials from two different cars. For this new car to be built well, it must be on a supporting surface that supports parts from both original cars. There will be a process of planning and drawing up blueprints. Parts, tools, and accessories will need to be sourced. The building of the complex components and bodywork modifications will need to be done, and the different parts will need to be tested to make sure they fit and work safely. The balancing and alignment of the wheels will require a surface that can take the weight of the entire new car that is being built.

Your marriage is like that classic car. You're coming together with your dents and scrapes. Your supporting surface is a nourishing community that not only supports you through the wedding planning and celebration stage but supports the now united YOU (both of you). The parts, tools, and accessories you need to build a healthy marriage are most likely available in a nourishing community. When normal challenges arise because of your inherent differences, this community will help you ensure things are working as they should, helping you both to balance and align.

We attribute the fact that we didn't make a total mess of our marriage within our first two years to finding ourselves in a community that nurtured marriages. We had more experienced couples who were willing to let their experiences and hindsight become our foresight. Like many people, we had traumas and negative experiences from our homes of origin and individual life experiences. We were just fortunate to have had mentors who guided us by sharing their own experiences.

"Mentoring is a brain to pick, an ear to listen, and a push in the right direction."
—John C. Crosby

Activity 2 (10 minutes)

Do this individually.

A. Think about your relationship and evaluate if you have a community around you that supports the united YOU.

• Make a list of the individuals that you believe you can turn to as a couple when you need balancing and alignment in your relationship.

MAKE NOTES:

B. Share with your partner the names you came up with.

• Do you have names in common on your list?

MAKE NOTES:

If you find that you don't have anyone on your lists that you both agree will support the united YOU without taking sides or being biased, then it's time to get proactive.

Suggestion: Identify experienced couples whom you both know and believe are living a healthy marriage/relationship in your sphere of influence. Make yourselves available for a relationship with these couples.

> "Learn from the stories of people who faced the challenges you haven't yet experienced."
> —Joanna Barsh

Planning and drawing up blueprints

It's time to think about how you're going to build a solid, functional, healthy, safe, got-a-lot-of-life-in-it marriage. Drawing up blueprints requires dreaming.

Dreaming together will have a powerful effect on your relationship. Dreaming about your future family, career move, house, holiday, or goals can help to relieve some of the stresses of today.

Importance of dreaming together:

- It gives you something to connect over.

- It strengthens your commitment to each other.

- It gives you something to look forward to together.

- It gives you a goal to work toward together, thereby nurturing your partnership and strengthening your unity and teamwork.

- It creates an opportunity to develop intimacy, as it allows you a glimpse into your partner's innermost thoughts and feelings.

- It supports intentional living by helping you to clarify what's important to you as a couple.

- It may reawaken your passion for each other. The act of thinking about what you can accomplish together can be exciting and energizing.

Dreaming together is an opportunity for you to share some details of your present and future hopes for your marriage.

"If eyes are the window to the soul, then dreams are the back door to the heart."
—Reed Logan Westgate

Activity 3 (20 minutes)

Do this together.

Talk about the current state of your relationship, with a focus on what you want for your relationship tomorrow.

A.   What pressures are you facing right now in your relationship?

Acknowledge your current relationship experiences and admit the feelings that those experiences bring out in you.

See the Appendix 1 on page 161 for a list of feeling words.

MAKE NOTES:

Admit how current pressures are impacting your relationship.

Ask your partner this:

"What can I do to make your relationship experience tomorrow better than it was today?"

"What can I do to support you with the pressures you're facing right now?"

MAKE NOTES:

Act: Be committed to making changes, even if it's one small change at a time.

Think about practical ways you can support your partner to make tomorrow's relationship experience better than it was today.

MAKE NOTES:

> "A journey of a thousand miles begins with a single step."
>
> —Laozi

Activity 4　(30 minutes)

Do activities 4A individually and 4B-D together.

Where do you want your relationship to be in one year?

Examples of things you can think about include spirituality, communication, forgiveness, intimacy, etc.

What dreams do you have for your relationship in one year?

This could be projects you'd like to do together, a family holiday you'd like to go on, a home you'd like to buy, etc.

Activity Guide:

    A. Make a list of the things you as an individual want and hope for your relationship over the next year.

MAKE NOTES:

    B. Share your dreams. Talk about why this dream is important to you.

    C. Identify where your dreams intersect.

MAKE NOTES:

Create a joint plan for your common dreams and how you can achieve them together. You both must be committed to taking daily steps to actualize this dream.

MAKE NOTES:

"Alone we can do so little. Together we can do so much."

—Helen Keller

Growing together as a couple is an essential goal for your relationship.

Tips for growing together:

1. Have new experiences together. When you allow yourself to have uncomfortable experiences, you provide opportunities to be vulnerable with one another and grow in your relationship. Discomfort is inherent in growth. [2] When you embrace engaging in something that makes you uncomfortable, you motivate yourself and your partner to develop a closer relationship and build a lasting memory together. [3, 4] Be sure to pick something new for both of you.

2. Learn together by listening to podcasts together, taking some classes together, or reading a book. This means your minds are getting stimulated at the same time and you're growing intellectual closeness.

3. Serve together. This allows you to accomplish something meaningful, have fun together, and have an amazing growth experience. Identify something you both care about and take action to serve in a mutually agreed area of need. Be sure to set clear expectations about the purpose of your serving and agree on how long you'll serve in that area and how often.

Continued Activity

Take time this week to debrief on your experiences of the first part of this couples' guide.

Identify areas in your relationship that you both want to grow in.

What can you do that will facilitate this growing together?

Together, put plans in place to make it happen.

See the next page for some ideas to facilitate your conversation.

"Where there's no progress, there's no growth. If there's no growth, there's no life. Environment's void of change is eventually void of life."
—Andy Stanley

Twenty Conversations to Enhance Reconnection

1. Can we synchronize our calendars for the next week?

2. What's on your agenda for the coming week that I can support you with?

3. Do you have board game ideas from your childhood that we can incorporate into our collection? What board games do you like to play?

4. What was a high in your day today and what was a low point?

5. What do you think of the idea of disconnecting from our phones daily between 6:00 and 8:00 p.m. (set your own daily two-hour time frame) to fully reconnect with each other and as a family without outside interference?

6. Do you find it easy to tell me when you're feeling overwhelmed or flooded? If not, can you please help me to understand why not?

7. How can we foster a sense of adventure in our lives?

8. In what ways can we serve in our community to give back?

9. In what ways and how often do you like to stay connected when we're apart during the workday or when one of us is travelling? Text messages, phone calls?

10. What errands do you currently have to do that you don't like doing?

11. What can we learn to do together? (e.g., swimming, skating, dancing, riding a bicycle, etc.)

12. What adventures would you like us to try in the next year?

13. What would our day look like if we got our child(ren) ready for school together and prepared meals together in the evening?

14. How often can we afford to go on dates at this time?

15. What would it look like for us to say goodbye and hello with connection in mind? A kiss and a hug, turning toward each other to say bye and hello?

16. What would our relationship look like if we went to sleep at the same time, if we woke up in the morning at the same time, or if we got ready for bed at the same time?

17. How do you currently deal with hard days or an experience of bad luck?

18. How do you like to be renewed when you feel tired/ fatigued or burned out?

19. How do you like to celebrate birthdays, anniversaries, and holidays? Do you like intimate celebrations of just our family, a small gathering of friends, or a big party at home or a separate venue?

20. Do you like to bring friends to our home? How often?

CHAPTER 2

WHAT IS YOUR
Communication
STYLE?

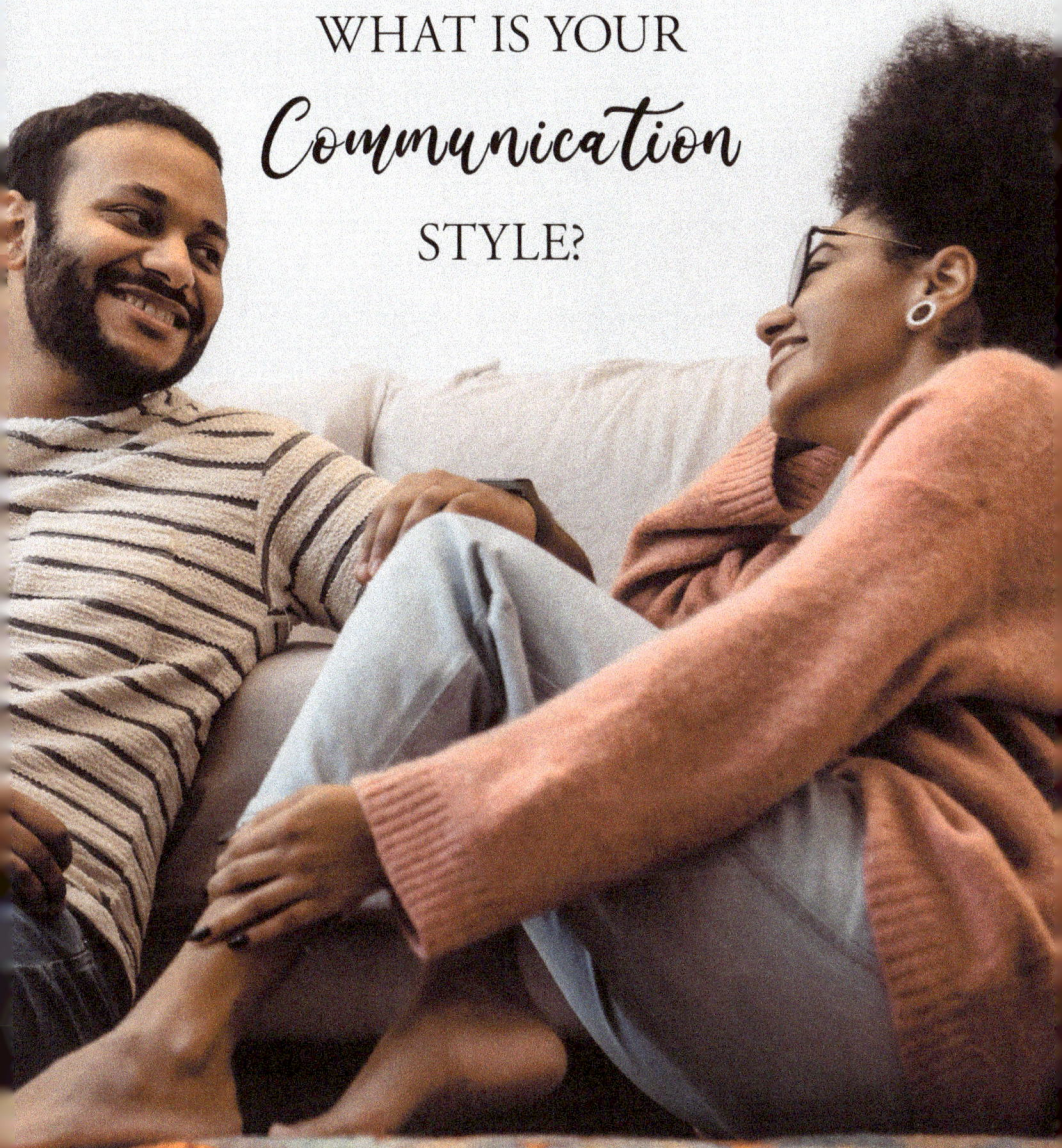

No one is born with an innate ability to communicate perfectly. Your communication style is influenced by your personality, life experiences, and general worldview. Good communication, however, is essential for a healthy relationship.

The basic communication styles are identified here, and examples of how this could play out in your relationship are provided.

There are four main communication styles that you might fit into.[5]

1. **Passive communicator.** This entails a person not expressing their feelings or needs, ignoring what's good for them, and allowing their partner to do the same. This person will defer to their partner for all decision-making to avoid tension or conflict. This person likely has a victimhood mindset. Inevitably, this type of communication will lead to built-up anger or resentment over time.

   If you find yourself almost always saying things like:

   "I'm okay with whatever you want, decide, want or do,"

   "Your idea is way better; mine wouldn't have been great anyway,"

   without making eye contact or while looking down, you're likely employing passive communication in your relationship.

2. **Aggressive communicator.** This person is likely to attack or confront in a conversation with hostile, antagonistic, or belligerent behavior. They'll communicate their point and defend their interests forcefully. In a relationship, this could mean an aggressive communicator expressing their ideas, feelings, and needs at the expense of their partner's feelings. When confronted, they'll get defensive or hostile. This communication style over time will likely cause your partner to feel alienated and hurt.

If you find yourself making statements like:

"This is what we're going to do, and that's that, so get over it,"

"It's your fault this is happening right now,"

with body language that involves crossing your arms, eye-rolling, yelling, raising of voice, or finger-pointing, you're likely employing aggressive communication in your relationship.

3. **Passive-aggressive communicator.** This communication style usually has the appearance of passivity on the surface, but there are subtle signs that anger is being acted out. The person using this form of communication will often use sarcasm or indirect communication or avoid communication in total. This person will have limited consideration for their partner's rights, needs, and feelings and will often use the "silent treatment" to try to make a point.

If you find yourself making statements like:

"No offense, but …,"

"There's nothing to be upset about here, so why are you getting so upset?"

with body language that expresses disdain, like sneering or eye-rolling, you're likely employing passive-aggressive communication in your relationship.

4. **Assertive communicator.** This person will be direct and honest in their communication about thoughts and feelings. They can respect the ideas, needs, and feelings of their partner while also asserting their own.

If you find that when speaking with your partner, your statements sound something like:

"I feel … when you … and I need for you to help me …,"

while making eye contact with your partner with a relaxed posture, you're likely using an assertive communication style.

Activity 1 (15 minutes)

Read through the list of statements and, using the scale below, write the number you believe corresponds to you (if you're likely or not to say something like that).

Review your communication style. Please do this on your own.

When communicating with my partner, I'm likely to or may have used this statement or one similar, or just had the thought in my head:

0. **never true**   1. **rarely true**   2. **sometimes true**

3. **usually true**   4. **almost always true**

1. Please don't walk away from me while we're having a conversation. □

2. Sure, we can do things your way (then you mutter to yourself). □

3. There's nothing I can do about it. □

4. I'm right and you're wrong. □

5. You're right, I shouldn't feel like that. □

6. I feel hurt when I … because you did … □

7. I don't care what you have to say. □

8. Why are you getting so upset? □

9. This isn't a priority for me. Can we look at another time we might both be able to … □

10. This is all your fault. ☐

11. I guess I should listen to you because you're so much smarter than I am. ☐

12. If that's what you want to do. ☐

13. I disagree with that. I see it this way … ☐

14. You owe me. ☐

15. I feel overburdened when you don't pitch in and help keep the house clean and tidy. ☐

16. That's not my responsibility. ☐

17. You never consider my feelings. ☐

18. You're the only one who can help me. ☐

19. I know you didn't mean it, but I feel offended by your comment. ☐

20. I don't agree with you, so I don't have to listen to your opinion. ☐

21. I feel sad when I come home, and you don't seem happy to see me or ask how my day was. ☐

22. Go ahead, my contribution to the conversation wasn't important anyway. ☐

23. You should have known that. ☐

24. You never do anything right. ☐

25. I just want to keep the peace. ☐

26. No offense, but … ☐

27. I'll get my way no matter what. ☐

28. It really doesn't matter that much. ☐

29. You must do what I say. ☐

30. You're too sensitive. ☐

31. I see that you're angry. I hear you saying that …; however, I disagree with you, and here's why... ☐

32. I'm not sure I can help you. ☐

Results of Reviewing Your Communication Style

A. Add up your scores from the statements as follows:

Communication Style	My Score	Partner's Score
Aggressive (statements 4, 7, 10, 14, 20, 24, 27, 29)		
Passive Aggressive (statements 2, 8, 12, 16, 18, 23, 26, 30)		
Passive (statements 3, 5, 11, 17, 22, 25, 28, 32)		
Assertive (statements 1, 6, 9, 13, 15, 19, 21, 31)		

B. **Individual Reflection**.

If you've done the exercise above as honestly as possible, you will have identified the communication style you've been using in your relationship.

Knowing what you've just learned about the different communication styles, acknowledge to yourself how your communication style may have played a positive or negative role in your relationship.

Good Communication

Regardless of the communication style you've used to date, everyone needs to learn the art of good communication. Good communication is essential for a healthy relationship.

What is good communication?

Good communication is the transfer of information or the sharing of feelings to another person, where both parties feel safe, heard, and not judged.

Layers of Communication

- **Verbal communication:** Don't underestimate the power of spoken words. They can hurt, or they can heal.

- **Nonverbal communication:** Your tone of voice and body language matter. Your facial expressions, hand gestures, and posture communicate to your partner if they're safe, heard, and not judged.

- **Visual communication:** Your partner can see if you're interested in them or not, and if they're safe or not.

"Good communication is the bridge between confusion and clarity."
—Nat Turner

Four Levels of Communication.

Your communication must involve all four levels [6] for your relationship to thrive.

1. **Superficial:** This communication is limited to unimportant chit-chat, where nothing said is particularly useful or consequential to either party. Important topics are never raised in superficial communication.

    Examples:

    "Some weather out there today."

    "What's for dinner?"

2. **Sharing facts:** This level of communication is comfortable and non-threatening, with some basic facts being shared.

    Examples:

    "The weather out there is too cold/hot."

    "We need to prepare dinner."

3. **Opinion level:** Here you start to share your ideas and opinions about facts. At this level, you can dig deeper into what the facts mean to you and your partner.

    Example 1:

    "The weather is too hot, and I think the temperature is going to burn my skin if I don't put on sunscreen."

    This opens an opportunity for your partner to pass you the sunscreen and perhaps offer to rub it on your back.

    Example 2:

    "We need to make dinner, and I think we should cook fish. Would you like that, or do you have another preference?"

    This allows your partner to give their opinion about your suggestions, and perhaps make some suggestions of their own.

4. **Feeling level:** This is where emotions and needs are shared. Levels 1–3 are essential in a relationship. However, for a

relationship to be healthy and thriving, level 4 is absolutely required. This is because the feeling level of communication is where you communicate how the facts have affected you personally, and it takes *vulnerability* and *courage*.

Example 1:

"The weather is too hot, and I think the temperature is going to burn my skin if I don't put on sunscreen. Could you rub some sunscreen on my back for me please; it feels good when you do it."

Example 2:

"We need to make dinner, and I'd like for us to do it together. It would allow us to catch up on our day, and I'd like that."

"Until a person knows your feelings, he/she doesn't really know you."
—Dr Alan Zimmerman

The definitions of vulnerability and courage we're adopting here are:

> "**Vulnerability** is the willingness to show emotions or allow one's weaknesses to be seen or known; a willingness to risk being emotionally hurt."[7]

> "**Courage** is the deliberate choice and willingness to face something, confront, express or feel something that could be painful or fearful for the sake of a worthy goal."[8]

If you're willing to be courageous and allow vulnerability in your relationship, your communication at the feelings level will allow you to be seen and known for the worthy goal of developing deep intimacy and trust in your relationship.

All four levels of communication are essential in a thriving relationship.

"There is no courage without vulnerability, uncertainty, risk, and emotional exposure."
—Brené Brown

How to communicate well.

- Timing is key: It's important to choose an appropriate time to bring up an important issue at the fact and feeling level of communication. Ensure that there are no distractions and ask your partner if it's a good time to talk. Be sure to respect their answer.

- Choose only one issue per sitting: You may have several issues to discuss; however, you must focus on one topic per sitting. This enables your partner to process a singular issue and be able to respond clearly and come up with ideas on how to change or manage the issue.

- Use "I" statements, combined with the behavior, situation, and feeling(s) attached to the experience.

- Example: "I felt frustrated and unseen when I came home from work, and you continued playing the game and stayed on the sofa for hours without paying any attention to my presence."

"Excellent communication doesn't just happen naturally. It is a product of process, skill, climate, relationship, and hard work."
—Pat McMillan

The Art of Listening.

Listening is something you consciously choose to do. It requires you to concentrate fully on what your partner is saying so that your brain can process the meaning of what's being said. Listening leads to learning; hearing is just the perception of sound. If you listen to your partner, you'll learn about them.

While listening to your partner, if your inner dialogue is about anything other than a heart posture that seeks to understand, your response is not likely to meet the needs of your partner. Many people listen with the view of formulating their response, which inevitably leads to conflict because the partner's need hasn't been met, due to a lack of understanding.

The great news is that listening skills can be learned and refined.

How to Listen Well.

- Eliminate distractions: To listen actively, you must be intentional to remove anything that could distract your mind from concentrating on what your partner is saying.

- Use verbal and non-verbal cues by leaning in, making eye contact, smiling, or nodding where appropriate to encourage your partner to continue.

- Withhold any judgment, even in your mind.

- Ask clarifying questions. Clarifying questions help to remove ambiguity, elicit additional details, and help you to understand what your partner is saying.

- Summarize and repeat back to your partner what they've said. You will paraphrase what you think you've heard them say.

   This isn't an opportunity for you to get passive-aggressive with a statement like, "So, let me get this straight."

   Instead, you could try, "I heard that … Is this correct?"

Activity 2 (40 minutes)

Do this together.

Practice communicating well and the art of listening.

A. Ask your partner, "In what ways has my communication style hurt you or not been beneficial to our relationship? (The idea is to allow each other to discuss issues that may have arisen because of your communication styles.)

Decide which of you will go first.

The role of the listener during this time is to:

1 Make clear eye contact.

2 Lean in and keep an open posture. Note, that folding your arms across your chest is not an open posture.

3 Nod or smile appropriately to encourage your partner to continue talking.

4 Check your inner dialogue. When your inner voice starts to construct a counter argument you may want to speak out over your partner, interrupting them, tap your knee, and remain silent.

E. When your partner has finished talking, ask any clarifying questions you may have.

F. Summarize what you heard your partner tell you by paraphrasing. It's important not to add your feelings, thoughts, or responses at this time.

G. Encourage your partner to clarify anything significant that they think you have missed.

H. Check your perception by asking your partner, "Did I hear that you're feeling ABC with me, because of how I've been communicating?"

I.   This will allow your partner to clarify the emotional aspects of this conversation.

J.   Empathize with your partner. Empathy is the ability to sense other people's emotions coupled with the ability to imagine what that person might be feeling.

K.   Put yourself in your partner's shoes and try to understand what they're going through because of your communication style. The aim is for you to try to understand your partner's experience and perspective.

L.   Swap roles.

Continuing Activity

Consistency and repetition are important when learning new skills.

Over the next week, set two hours aside when you can practice the skills outlined in pages 29-30.

Choose an issue you need to discuss and follow the steps to communicate and listen well.

"Communication works for those who work at it."
—John Powell

CHAPTER 3

THAT CONFLICT
YOU LEFT
Unmanaged

Every relationship will experience conflict at one point or another. This isn't because you married the wrong person, and your relationship isn't doomed because you have conflict.

Conflict often reveals a few things in a relationship, like:

- different desires
- different priorities
- different backgrounds
- different personalities
- different value systems

Managing conflict doesn't always mean that you're going to solve the problem. It means that:

1. You're going to be prepared to acknowledge that there's an issue causing the conflict and be willing to talk about it respectfully.

2. You're going to be open-minded so that you can gain an awareness of how this issue impacts your partner.

3. You're going to be ready to act in a way that shows your partner that you're trying to understand their perspective and de-escalate the conflict. This would involve open body language, a nod, eye contact, or even an offer of physical affection, like handholding.

Conflict provides a valuable opportunity to learn about your partner's past emotional injuries (also known as triggers), values, needs, desires, priorities, and unique personality.

Negative Ways to Handle Conflict

- Jumping to conclusions and guessing at motives rather than finding out the facts and the feelings.

- Judging your partner and assigning negative labels to them rather than just naming the behavior.

- Trying to win the conversation and defeat your partner rather than trying to understand.

- Bringing up the past rather than talking about present issues.

- Bringing up minor problems to bulk up a major problem.

- Refusing to see that it's okay to have differences in opinions and refusing to talk about these differences.

- Using "You are" statements rather than "I feel" statements.

- Using the silent treatment. This is particularly damaging to a relationship.

"In every complaint, there is a dream, a wish, a request."
—Dr Gottman

Food for thought

Can you see the dream, wish, or request that your partner is trying to communicate in the issue causing conflict in your relationship?

Impact of the Silent Treatment on Your Relationship

The silent treatment is defined as an act of completely ignoring a person by resorting to silence, especially as a means of expressing contempt or disapproval.[9] This is a form of aggression and is often used as a manipulative tactic or by a partner who feels like the other partner is unwilling to meet their need. This can be distressing for the partner on the receiving end of silent and cold treatment.

The feelings the silent treatment elicits could include:

- anger
- confusion
- frustration
- worthlessness
- feeling unloved

Over time, these negative feelings will deteriorate a relationship to a point where it's simply unsustainable.

If you are the partner using the silent treatment, it's time to stop damaging your relationship and start repairing it. Acknowledge to your spouse that you've been guilty of hurting your relationship with silent and cold treatment. Apologize and share that you want to change, and that you'd like to get some help. Use this couples' guide as a start; however, we recommend that you get marriage counselling or coaching.

> "The silent treatment: A deadly killer of friendship."
> —Peter Jackson

Three Tips for Managing Conflict: Acknowledge, Awareness, and Action

1. **Acknowledge your differences:** By now you may have realized that some of the things that have caused conflict in your relationship are because of your fundamental differences. If not, the activity below will give you an idea about some of the differences in your personality, temperament, values, and upbringing.

Activity 1   (5 minutes)

Learn your differences to be able to lend your strengths to one another.

Put your initials in the box, thinking about the way you are most of the time.

Example: Ife = I, Dami = D

	D			I	
Activities	I prefer planning.			I prefer to be spontaneous.	
	I			D	
Communication	I get straight to the point.			I explain the broader details.	

Your Turn: Put your initials where you fall in the box.

Please do this individually.

Activities	I prefer planning.			I prefer to be spontaneous.	
Communication	I get straight to the point.			I explain the broader details.	
Decisions	I let my heart lead.			I use logic.	
Disagreements	I prefer to confront the issues.			I prefer to keep the peace.	

Decisions	I let my heart lead.	I use logic.
Disagreements	I prefer to confront the issues.	I prefer to keep the peace.
Expressing Love	My partner knows I love them. I don't have to say it often.	I say "I love you" often. I feel it is important.
Feelings	I find it easy to express my feelings.	I find it hard to express my feelings.
Money	I love to spend more than to save.	I love to save more than to spend.
People	I prefer to spend time alone.	I prefer time with others.
Planning	I like to live in the moment.	I like to plan for the future.

Problem solving	I buy a book, listen to podcasts, or read a manual to find solutions.	I try to find solutions by trial and error.
Punctuality	I need to be on time.	I don't worry if we are late.
Interpersonal relations	I am charming and impulsive.	I am prepared, reliable, and organized.
Relationship problems	I like to find new ways to solve problems.	I like to use the solutions we've used before.
Sleep	I like to go to sleep early.	I like to go to sleep late.
Tidiness	I prefer everything to be in its place.	I don't mind a little mess, so long as we're having fun.

Activity 2 (20 minutes)

- **Do this together.** Show each other what you've noted with your initial on the scale above. Make a note in the scale in your journal where your partner placed themselves and see where there are differences.

- Share with your partner why you think you fall where you do on the scale, especially in those areas where you are opposites.

- How did your upbringing play a role in these dispositions?

- Together, identify one area in which your differences may have caused you to disagree. Think of how these differences can be a source of strength for your relationship. Come up with different scenarios and discuss them.

Three Tips for Managing Conflict (continued)

2. **Have a conversation about the issue:** Respectful and open conversation about issues causing conflict without criticism, contempt, stonewalling, and defensiveness is an important step in managing conflict. Conversation brings about an awareness of the heart of the conflict.

"Where your partner is weaker and you're strong, you lend your strength to the relationship."
—Ife and Dami Adingupu

Activity 3 (30 minutes)

Each of you should choose your point of conflict that you've left unmanaged. Take turns to speak and listen using skills learned in Chapter 2.

MY ISSUE:

YOUR ISSUE:

Decide who goes first and take turns addressing the issue one at a time.

- The speaker must communicate honestly and clearly about that singular issue. Share your perspective about the issue, perhaps where that perspective comes from, what triggered the conflict, what the issue means for you, what desires or needs are not being met, and what you're afraid of losing. You could adapt this model " " statement:

    a   I feel (describe your strongest feeling)

    b   When you (description of the behavior/issue)

    c   Because (the specific impact or consequences)

- The listener must listen without judgment. When your partner has finished, ask clarifying questions, and summarize what you've heard by paraphrasing.

- Brainstorm together possible solutions, using sentences like:

  a   I would like (what you want your partner to do in the future to prevent the problem).

  b   We could try XYZ. Think of creative ideas to help you move your positions toward each other. You each probably have a unique point of view, so being right isn't the goal.

WRITE DOWN THE IDEAS/ SOLUTIONS:

Choose the other issue and follow the same process.

If you find that emotions are running high and you're not able to come up with ideas right now, take a break but commit to revisiting this issue in __minutes/hours.

Note that you need at least 20 minutes to regulate physiologically and neurologically, so take at least a 20-minute break.

How to Call Timeout Effectively

Calling timeout during a disagreement can save your relationship. We acknowledge that it can be a difficult thing to do because it takes a lot of self-discipline for both partners and can also be used in an abusive way to shut down each other or to refuse to engage in a difficult discussion. However, there are physiological advantages to calling a timeout in an escalating conflict.

When you start to feel overwhelmed in a disagreement, the loving part of your brain shuts off (known as emotional flooding)[10] and the fight or flight part of your brain takes over. Timeout helps your brain to reset and allows the loving part to reactivate. At the very basic level, your heart rate is likely going to go up and your blood pressure will increase in an escalating conflict. Taking a break will help these systems to calm down so that they can return to your baseline.

Steps for effective timeout:

    A. At a time when your relationship is in a good place, agree on what your "I need a timeout" cue will be during conflict. It can be a signal or words.

    B. Identify what triggers an escalation in your disagreement and be intentional in avoiding these (e.g., name-calling, blaming, shaming, "you" statements).

    C. Agree on how long your timeout will be for. You need at least 20 minutes. Communicate this to your spouse during conflict.

        Example: "I need a break. I'm feeling overwhelmed. Can we resume this in 30 minutes please?"

    D. Respect your spouse when they ask for a timeout. Don't think "I have to say this last thing" or utter one more hurtful word.

    E. During your timeout, take deep breaths. Acknowledge to yourself the main reasons you're upset, but also remind yourself of the positive attributes of your spouse. Be careful to take responsibility for anything you may have done or said to contribute to the current escalation of the disagreement.

    F. Come back at the set time to resume discussion of the issue.

Three Tips for Managing Conflict (continued)

3. **Focus on the future:** Using the **acknowledge**, **aware**, and **act** template, you have now acknowledged that there are points of conflict that you need to manage in your relationship, and you should also be aware of how these issues affect each person.

   It's important to not dwell on the past and recognize that while the past can't be changed, you can create a plan to address the conflict so that you can have the type of future you want.

   The **acting** part of this requires you to individually think of positive steps you can take to address the issues you've been discussing. Then do this intentionally and consistently.

Activity 4 (5 minutes)

Individual Reflection

What can you do this week that will be a reparative action(s) for the conflict you've been discussing?

MAKE NOTES:

> "Conflict can destroy a team which hasn't spent time learning to deal with it."
>   —Thomas Isgar

Continued Activity

There may be other areas of conflict that you were unable to address during Activity 3 above.

We encourage you to identify those areas of conflict, write them down, and then together set a date and at least a two-hour window when you can address these issues using the skills learned in Chapters 2 and 3.

MAKE NOTES:

CHAPTER 4

Forgiving

WHAT YOUR BRAIN
WON'T FORGET

We all at some point in our relationship have hurt our partners. For you to have a healthy relationship, it's important to identify the areas where you've been hurt and need forgiveness. And for the transgressor, it's important to acknowledge that you have hurt your partner, accept the damage this may have done to your relationship, and act in a consistent way to mitigate the effect of the transgression.

You've probably heard the axiom "time heals all wounds." The common misconception is that even if you do nothing, the wound caused by a transgression will be healed with time. While forgiveness may become more likely as time distances you from the transgression, time does not heal the wound by itself if the necessary work to bring forgiveness and healing isn't done.

When you remember an event that caused you emotional hurt, you may feel like the event occurred closer or farther away in time. This is an important factor in your willingness to forgive a transgression, perhaps because you've been able to distance yourself from that event that caused you emotional pain—or not. [11] Another factor is the affection and the attachment you have for the offender, as this will determine the degree of pain you feel from the hurt. So, the emotional wound caused by your partner doesn't heal without you intentionally working on those areas where you've been wounded.

The good news is that forgiveness is a skill that can be learned, and it will transform your relationship.

"It has been said time heals all wounds. I do not agree. The wounds remain. In time the mind protecting its sanity covers them with scar tissue and pain lessens. But it is never gone."
—Rose Kennedy

Activity 1 (5 minutes)

Individual Reflection

Think about an event that occurred within your relationship that caused you emotional pain.

When this event comes to mind, do you *feel* that the event is closer or farther away in time?

Write your reflections about the event:

- What was the event?
- What feelings do you have about this event?

MAKE NOTES:

Reactions to Hurt

Most people react to hurt in one of two ways—avoidance or grudge-holding/revenge.[12] Both reactions result in negative behaviors.

Activity 2   (15 minutes)

A. **Do this individually.** Identify how you react to hurt.

Think about the event you identified in **Activity 1** and select which of the statements below describes your possible reaction.

When I think of the event that caused me hurt, I am likely to:

0. **never true**   1. **rarely true**   2. **sometimes true**

3. **usually true**   4. **almost always true**

1. Withdraw from my partner	☐
2. Become hostile and irritable	☐
3. Have thoughts of how I can get back at my partner	☐
4. Go out of my way to avoid my partner if I think the issue will be brought up	☐
5. Start to worry excessively	☐
6. Ruminate repeatedly on the events that caused me to hurt	☐
7. Do something, even if very little, that I know will hurt my partner	☐
8. Notice a change in my sleep pattern	☐
9. Feel overwhelmed, helpless, or hopeless	☐

10. Be unable to empathize if I see my partner struggling/ hurting and I remember what they did to hurt me ☐

11. Refuse to admit that I am hurt or angry ☐

12. Bring up the issue in a confrontation ☐

13. Give my partner the silent treatment ☐

14. Become controlling ☐

15. Become cold and sarcastic ☐

16. Withhold affection and/or sex ☐

Add your scores to the questions according to the table below:

Reaction to hurt	My score	Partner's score
Avoidant coping (statements 1,4,5,8,9,11,13,16)		
Revengeful coping (statements 2,3,6,7,10,12,14,15)		

Use the scale below to see where you currently fall (write your scores where they fall in the scale).

	0–10	>10–21	>21–32
	Low	**Moderate**	**Extreme**
Avoidant coping			
Revengeful coping			

There is a maximum of 32 points for each coping style. In a healthy relationship, both partners need to be on the low end of this scale. This indicates that occasionally in our humanness we will respond to hurt using avoidant or revengeful coping. There must be awareness that this can be the case and you must take steps to repair these negative ways of responding in your relationship.

If you find that you scored in the moderate to extreme end of the scale, it's important to take this awareness and move into acknowledging that this way of responding to hurt sometimes, usually, and almost always will further impact your relationship negatively. Both partners must act in ways that will move the relationship to a place that is healthy.

Activity 2B below will get you started on moving your relationship to a place where you're responding to hurt with healthy responses.

B. Look at each other's scores and discuss how your current individual style of coping with hurt may have resulted in further hurt in your relationship.

Forgiveness Is the Key

The activity above is to help you acknowledge the way you may have been coping with hurt in your relationship. The truth is that regardless of your coping style, the perception that you've been wronged or treated unfairly naturally results in anger. Anger in itself isn't a bad thing. You can use anger as an indicator that something is wrong emotionally and needs to be dealt with.

To recognize how you're currently dealing with anger, we recommend a quiz on anger assessment designed by Dr. Gray Chapman:

https://5lovelanguages.com/quizzes/anger-assessment

(*The 5 Love Languages* ®: *The Secret to Love that Lasts* by Dr. Gary Chapman)

What Is Forgiveness?

Forgiveness is not excusing, exonerating, justifying, condoning, or pardoning.

Forgiveness is a *continued process* of voluntary transformation of your feelings, attitudes, and behavior toward the person who wronged you so that you are no longer dominated by negative resentment-based emotions, motivations, and reasoning and can express compassion, generosity, or the like. [13]

Forgiveness must happen to reduce the motivation to avoid the transgressor or to seek revenge. Without forgiveness, your relationship can't move forward healthily. This is also important because forgiveness not only benefits your relationship, but it also has mental and physical benefits for you. [14]

"Love prospers when a fault is forgiven but dwelling on it separates close friends."
—Solomon, king of Israel, ~967–931 B.C.

Forgiveness requires you to decide and involves your emotions

To move past your current way of coping with hurt, you must decide to forgive and change the emotional responses associated with the feelings of hurt.

Experts say there are two types of forgiveness: [12]

- **Decisional forgiveness:** This is a behavioral intention to resist an unforgiving stance and to respond differently toward your partner. This involves making a conscious decision to let go of hurt feelings like anger and resentment, putting them in the past, and moving forward free of the effects those feelings can bring.

- **Emotional forgiveness:** This is the replacement of negative, unforgiving emotions with positive-oriented emotions. This means you replace the negative emotions with ones like empathy, compassion, or sympathy.

Emotional, Physical, and Health Benefits of Forgiveness

Research has shown that there are several physical, emotional, and health benefits of forgiveness. [15, 16] These include:

1. lower blood pressure
2. improved heart health
3. improved self-esteem
4. healthier relationships
5. improved mental health
6. a stronger immune system
7. fewer symptoms of depression
8. less anxiety, stress, and hostility

Seven Practical Steps to Forgive

1. **Identify** the transgressions you would like to forgive.

2. **Acknowledge**

   a   how the transgression changed you, or the impact it had on you;

   b   that forgiving this transgression not only benefits your partner but also will be positive for you.

3. **Accept** that you can't change the past and your anger will not redeem what your partner has done.

Activity 3 (5 minutes)

Identify, Acknowledge, Accept

This is an individual reflection activity for you to identify a transgression by your partner that caused you hurt that you need to forgive.

This will be used in Activity 4.

How did this change or impact you?

Can you see ways in which forgiving this transgression can be beneficial for you, given that you can't change the past?

WRITE YOUR REFLECTIONS HERE:

Seven Practical Steps to Forgive (continued)

4. **Talk** about the transgression and the hurt it caused you, using the skills learned in Chapter 2.

   Recognize that even small transgressions that hurt your heart, if left unaddressed, can build up resentment in your heart. But when you bring hurt into the open, you stand a chance of the hurt being healed.

> "When you keep sweeping things under the carpet, eventually the lump is big enough for the auditors to trip over."
>
> —Bill Sanderson

Activity 4 (30 minutes)

Address Your Hurt

Do this together.

This activity concentrates on communicating the unaddressed hurt that a transgression caused you and helping your partner understand the feelings attached to it.

Activity 5 will focus on apology and forgiveness.

The cause of the hurt could be recent or a long time ago, and your partner might or might not have been aware of it. You can continue here with the transgression you identified in activity 3.

Make sure you use the "I" statements to describe your feelings.

Examples:

"I was hurt when I found out that you had a promotion at work and received a significant salary increase and you had hidden that from me."

"I haven't gotten over the fact that at the time I needed money to repair my car, you didn't offer to help me."

"I feel frustrated and unloved because it appears that you value money more than you do me."

- The listener must maintain appropriate eye contact and avoid interrupting the speaker.

- The listener must "echo back" to the speaker by paraphrasing the reason for their partner's hurt and the feelings associated with that hurt. There must be no interpretation of what was said or attempts at self-defence.

Example: "You feel frustrated and unloved because I hid my salary increase from you and didn't offer to help pay for your car repair."

You can ask clarifying questions like, "What did you mean by that?"

The listener can make notes about the ways you have hurt your partner.

- **Swap roles**: The partner who has not communicated their hurt must now do so without the listener interrupting.

Seven Practical Steps to Forgive (continued)

5. **Decide** to forgive. Whether you decide to forgive or not determines if you're able to progress to the remaining practical steps. This decision will also impact the quality of your relationship with your partner, or if your relationship will have a future at all.

6. **Emotional forgiveness**. This involves acts of kindness, kind words, and empathy.

7. **Consistent intentional repairing**. The hurt from the transgression will not go away overnight, and there may be scenarios that trigger the memory of it. When this happens, you must consistently and intentionally remind yourself that you already decided to forgive and replace whatever negative feelings that come with positive-oriented ones.

"Forgiveness is the final form of love."
—Reinhold Niebuhr

Six Practical Steps to Heal the Hurt You Caused

1. **Responsibility.** You need to take responsibility for how you have hurt your partner which could have negatively impacted your relationship and haven't been addressed. Identify a good time to have a conversation about unresolved hurt and take the initiative to bring it into the open. Ask yourself these questions:

- What have I failed to do that I should have been doing?

- What have I done or am I doing that I know I should not do?

- In what areas have I failed to meet my partner's needs?

- What have I said to my partner in the past that I know is hurtful?

- In what areas could I have communicated love to my partner that I have refused to?

    Reflections: Take some time this week to reflect and make a list of things that come to your mind. Be specific.

    Examples:

    "I haven't been listening to suggestions and advice my partner gives me; instead, I take my mother's advice and opinion into consideration."

    "I said some unkind things during our disagreements about money last week that were demeaning to my partner."

Make Notes:

Six Practical Steps to Heal the Hurt You Caused (continued)

2. **Understanding**: You must be focused on understanding the effect of your actions/behavior on your partner's feelings, rather than trying to justify your feelings. When you're the transgressor, your job is to cater to your partner's needs to ensure that their emotions are restored as well as can be under the circumstances.

3. **Say sorry genuinely**. You must genuinely feel bad about the issues that were identified and express this in your apology for your partner to believe you. This means you must take responsibility, acknowledge your mistakes, and make no excuses or blame your partner.

   Examples:

   Apology that makes excuses or blames:

   "I'm sorry that I talked down at you at the party last night, but you had drunk too much alcohol, and you know that I don't like you drinking."

   Proper apology:

   "I'm sorry that I talked down at you at the party last night. It was rude and disrespectful of me. Please forgive me."

"Never ruin an apology with an excuse."
—Benjamin Franklin

Activity 5   (20 minutes)

Apology and Forgiveness

A. Use the "Richter Scale" of hurt to find out how serious the hurt identified in Activity 4 is for your partner.

Take turns to do this.

Ask your partner: "What level on the Richter Scale is the hurt we discussed in Activity 4 for you?"

1: Insignificant	
2: Low	
3: Minor	
4: Moderate	
5: Intermediate	
6: Noteworthy	
7: High	
8: Far-reaching	
9: Outstanding	
10: Extraordinary	

This will create an awareness of the level of hurt that needs to be healed.

"It hurts because it matters."
—John Green

B. Take turns offering an apology to one another.

The apology: You can use the statement below as a guide.

I recognize (describe the transgression that) happened. Understandably, this hurt you (acknowledge the pain/ hurt that your action, behavior, or words caused your partner). I regret that this happened (express remorse or regret). Please forgive me (ask for forgiveness). In the future, I will (offer a remedy).

"If an apology is followed by an excuse or a reason, it means they are going to commit the same mistake again they just apologized for."
—Amit Kalantri

Six Practical Steps to Heal the Hurt You Caused (continued)

3. **Gestures**: Make gestures that indicate your remorse. If you have done the first three parts of this section well, then you may want to get creative to show gestures that indicate you are truly remorseful.

- It's important that you use your partner's apology language. To recognize your apology language, we recommend you attempt the quiz "apology language" by Dr. Gray Chapman.

    https://5lovelanguages.com/quizzes/apology-language

    (*The 5 Love Languages* ®: *The Secret to Love that Lasts* by Dr. Gary Chapman)

- Whether you write a note or buy flowers, be sure that this gesture is genuine to consistently reinforce that you are sorry.

4. **Be respectful**. Remember that forgiveness is not a one-time thing, and that it's a continued process until the hurt is healed. Be aware that your partner's forgiveness process is unique to them. You can't prescribe how they should feel because you have apologized, or how they should react to you. If you're respectful of your partner's process, your relationship stands a higher chance of being repaired and restored. Being respectful means:

    - If your partner needs a little space, you grant it.

    - If they want to talk it out, you listen and let them get out all their feelings.

    - You must put your partner's feelings first.

5. Consistent intentional repairing

Forgiveness is a continued process, not a singular action. This is because the brain doesn't just forget the event immediately when you decide to forgive or when you apologize. Repairing an emotional hurt takes consistent intentional actions that show your partner over time your true repentance and this can build trust.

You've probably heard the saying "forgive and forget." Forgetting likely doesn't happen when there's just hollow forgiveness based only on a decision without any action to replace the negative emotions with positive-oriented ones. When you combine decisional and emotional forgiveness, there's a higher chance of forgetting.

The concept of "forgive and forget" is a delicate one because it may have caused negative feelings or outcomes in the past, like:

- causing you to be isolated
- causing you to feel helpless
- causing feelings of guilt and shame
- causing you to feel or be revictimized
- resulting in prolonged or continued abuse

Please reach out to a mental health professional if you want to discuss further how these fit into your situation.

"Forgiveness does not change the past, but it does enlarge the future."
—Paul Boose

Continued Activity

- Over the next weeks and to continuously repair and reconnect to each other, think about gestures you can use to show your partner that you're remorseful about the issues you've discussed, and then do it.

- Think about how you can be respectful of your partner's forgiveness and healing process.

- Think about other issues that have resulted in hurt in your relationship that need to be forgiven. Use the skills learned so far to address these. Remember that when issues are brought to the open, the opportunity for healing and repair becomes possible.

CHAPTER 5

Marriage Is a Duet:

THE IMPACT OF GOOD AND BAD BACKUP SINGERS

Your Marriage is a duet that is influenced by many backup singers. These singers could be your background and past experiences from your home of origin or lived experiences. These impact the messages that are written on your heart, which in turn influences your personality, preferences, behaviors, and thoughts. The current influence your extended family has on you can also play a positive or negative role in the quality of your relationship.

Making the transition from being a part of your family of origin to making your own family, independent from your family of origin, can be an exciting and challenging experience. It's important to recognize that your family background has a big impact on your relationship. Both the past and current impacts need to be considered.

Activity 1 (10 minutes)

A. Do this reflection individually.

What do you remember about your mom and dad's relationship?

MAKE NOTES:

B. Circle one of the images below that describes your parents' relationship as you remember it.

Dad   Mom   Dad   Mom

Dad Mom   Dad Mom

Adapted from the "Inclusion of the Other in the Self" (IOS) Scale, developed by Aron, Aron, and Smollan [17]

C. Compare your reflections with your partner's.

Family Factors That Shape Us

There are family factors that shape us as individuals and affect our personality and preferences. Recognizing how these family factors differ between you and your partner, and how they could be playing out in your relationship, is important for you to identify positive and negative effects.

These factors are about your experience with your parents or main caregiver(s): [18]

1. **Emotional Closeness:** This is the extent to which you experienced your parents' expressing closeness to each other, and how they helped and supported each other and you.

2. **Expressiveness:** This is your experience of how your parents encouraged you to express your choices and feelings openly or not, and how they modelled this.

3. **Conflict:** This is your experience of how the conflict(s) you experienced was dealt with, whether directly and openly, expressing their anger with aggression or the silent treatment. The way your parents modelled conflict management, whether with respect or disrespect, impacts how you manage conflict.

4. **Independence and Interdependence:** This is your experience with how your parents fostered independent thinking, decision-making, and problem-solving while encouraging collaborative working and supporting one another.

5. **Achievement:** This is the way your parents encouraged you to be achievement-oriented and/or competitive concerning school, sports, and careers or not. Your experience of how your parents celebrated one another's achievements or not also impacts your development.

6. **Culture:** This is the way your family was concerned with or participated in social, educational, intellectual, and cultural matters.

7. **Recreation:** This is the degree of importance your parents placed on sports, recreational activities, or leisure time.

8. **Morals and Religion:** This refers to your religious background and the importance your parents placed on religious practices and training in moral values.

9. **Organization:** This is your experience of things like planning, family meetings, finances, boundaries, and responsibility allocation within the family.

10. **Control:** This is how power, and authority were exercised by your parents.

In a healthy home, your experience of these 10 factors would have shaped you to be able to develop emotional closeness with your partner, express yourself with clarity and compassion, and manage conflict whilst being encouraging and collaborative in finding solutions or resolutions.

"A healthy home involves providing a secure base from which children can explore, and a safe haven to which they return to have their emotional needs met."
—Nicky and Sila Lee

Activity 2 (20 minutes)

Do this individually. Look back at your past to move forward. You'll bring a mixture of experiences from the ten factors listed above into your relationship. Think about your experiences from your home of origin and select relevant boxes that apply to you.

A. Reflect on your parents', stepparents', or main caregivers' relationship with you growing up.

Select all that applies to you.

Did your parents, stepparents, or main caregivers …

	Mother/ Stepmother / other female carer (✓ mark for Yes, and leave blank for No)	Father/ Stepfather/other male carers (✓ mark for Yes, and leave blank for No)
1. affirm you?	☐	☐
2. arrange playdates with peers for you in your home?	☐	☐
3. show you affection (e.g., hug/ kiss/ high-five you)?	☐	☐
4. play with you in a "peer-like" way, encouraging cooperative play?	☐	☐
5. show interest in you?	☐	☐

6. treat you equally to your siblings?	☐	☐
7. comfort you when you were upset?	☐	☐
8. set clear rules for you to follow?	☐	☐
9. celebrate your uniqueness?	☐	☐
10. have conversations with you and allow you to respond?	☐	☐
11. make you feel safe at home?	☐	☐
12. meet your physical needs, providing a home, food, clothes, etc.?	☐	☐
13. compliment you as a child?	☐	☐
14. explain safety rules to you often and consistently and model obedience to them (e.g., traffic light red means stop, green means go)?	☐	☐
15. encourage you to develop your interests?	☐	☐
16. discipline in a consistent way?	☐	☐
17. accept your friends?	☐	☐

18. allow you to have social interactions (e.g., go to movies with friends, parties, sleepovers)? ☐ ☐

19. set expectations that were appropriate for your age? ☐ ☐

20. say sorry to you when they made mistakes? ☐ ☐

21. show you examples of their own friendships and other relationships with persons outside your home? ☐ ☐

22. forgive you when you made mistakes? ☐ ☐

23. establish clear family rules? ☐ ☐

24. help you relate well with your siblings and peers? ☐ ☐

25. give you gifts? ☐ ☐

26. ask about your school day and interactions with your peers? ☐ ☐

27. take an interest in your academic achievement? ☐ ☐

28. give you a sense of security? ☐ ☐

Activity 2 (continued)

Do this individually.

B. Reflect on your parents', stepparents', or main caregivers' relationship with each other.

Did your parents, stepparents, or main caregivers ...

	Yes	Sometimes	No	Don't Know
show affection to each other?	☐	☐	☐	☐
have traditional roles?	☐	☐	☐	☐
express spontaneity?	☐	☐	☐	☐
show respect for one another?	☐	☐	☐	☐
show they trusted one another?	☐	☐	☐	☐
show they were committed to one another?	☐	☐	☐	☐
show kindness to each other?	☐	☐	☐	☐
have fun together regularly?	☐	☐	☐	☐
enjoy each other's company?	☐	☐	☐	☐
support each other's goals?	☐	☐	☐	☐
make decisions together?	☐	☐	☐	☐
have joint friends?	☐	☐	☐	☐
make money decisions together?	☐	☐	☐	☐
resolve conflict well?	☐	☐	☐	☐
have joint interests or hobbies?	☐	☐	☐	☐
communicate honestly and respectfully?	☐	☐	☐	☐

79

encourage each other with praise and affirmation?	☐	☐	☐	☐
say sorry and forgive each other?	☐	☐	☐	☐
show willingness to negotiate with each other?	☐	☐	☐	☐
listen well to each other without criticism and interruption?	☐	☐	☐	☐
help each other with small and big tasks?	☐	☐	☐	☐
remain faithful to each other?	☐	☐	☐	☐
give each other gifts?	☐	☐	☐	☐
show each other physical affection (e.g., hug/ kiss/ high-five)?	☐	☐	☐	☐
spend personal time together?	☐	☐	☐	☐
show they were interested in each other?	☐	☐	☐	☐
have a healthy loving relationship?	☐	☐	☐	☐

There are four major areas of development that children need to grow in:

1. Physical growth and feeling safe
2. Cognitive growth: your thinking, learning, and language
3. Emotional growth: feelings and emotions
4. Social growth: how you interact in and with society

All these areas are linked; therefore, development, or lack thereof, in one area affects the others.

"Children do learn what they live. Then they grow up to live what they've learned."
—Dorothy Nolte

Activity 2 (continued)

C. Evaluation and Reflection:

There are 14 points available for each of the four major areas of development that you needed as a child. Activity 2A above has 28 questions that cover those four major areas of development. Every mark ✓ Yes is worth 1 mark, and an unmarked sentence for either male or female influence is zero. Add up your scores as outlined in the table below.

	My Scores	Partner's Scores
Physical growth and feelings of safety Questions: 6, 8, 11, 12, 14, 16, 28		
Cognitive growth Questions: 5, 9, 15, 19, 23, 24, 27		
Emotional growth Questions: 1, 3, 7, 13, 20, 22, 25		
Social growth Questions: 2, 4, 10, 17, 18, 21, 26		

The lower your scores in any of the growth areas, the higher the likelihood that these areas were not nurtured in your formative years.

In combination, your answers in activities 1 and 2 should highlight to you if there were any area(s) where there might have been a lack.

If you experienced a lack, take time to acknowledge this and reflect to gain awareness on how this might have impacted you.

Activity 3 (30 minutes)

Together with your partner, review Activity 3a-g and discuss. Take turns discussing your individual experiences and perspectives.

A. Identify areas that you are grateful for from your upbringing and discuss these with your partner.

B. Discuss the areas of lack you recognize from Activity 2a with your partner.

   Listen, empathize, and comfort one another.

C. In what ways are the areas of lack that you identified currently negatively impacting your relationship?

   Listen to understand and empathize with each other.

D. Are there any area(s) in Activity 2a and 2b that you are currently imitating or would like to imitate and will be beneficial to your relationship?

MAKE NOTES:

E. Are there any area(s) in Activity 2b that you are currently imitating and are hurting your relationship and family?

MAKE NOTES:

F. Together, write out what you want for your relationship and family, combining the good things you identified in Activity 3D that you want to imitate and come up with new ideas to incorporate.

MAKE NOTES:

G. Think of actionable steps to do these things.

Example: We want to show more affection to each other and/or to our children.

Actionable step: Make a point to kiss good morning and good night every day and to check in with each other during the day to see how each other's day is going.

Set a reminder on your phone to remind you to send a "How are you, I miss you" text.

MAKE NOTES/ PLAN OF ACTION:

"If we fail to adapt, we fail to move forward."
—John Wooden

Current Impact of Family: Are They Good or Bad Backup Singers?

When you get married, you become a duo. While you must be in sync with one another, and act and live in unison, you must have people in your life who can provide support and community for your relationship. The primary place you get this is often from your family of origin. Your relationship with your extended family members can, however, become a source of conflict and stress for your marriage.

Problems with in-laws can be found in one of the following forms:

- Talking negatively about your partner.

- Interference with your marriage or family life by demanding information, giving advice, or pushing for certain outcomes or solutions.

- Abusive and toxic behaviors that may have been present when you were in your home of origin that continue after you get married. It's important to recognize what healthy behaviors are to be able to navigate this.

- Excessive demands for your resources. This usually happens in the case when a family puts pressure on one of you to support a sibling or their parents with their wants and needs.

"When you marry someone, you marry their entire family."

—Kevin Jonas

Activity 4   (20 minutes)

Do this individually.

A. Reflect on your relationship with your extended family.

Are there any areas where there's a lack of healthy boundaries? Is there undue influence, requests, or access to your relationship information, time, money, and/or decisions?

Are there any scenarios in which one of you is unduly inviting their parent(s) or extended family into your relationship by discussing or sharing your relationship information with them without your consent and/or despite your objections?

MAKE NOTES:

B. Share your notes with your partner.

Discuss any issues related to extended family that have caused you stress or are currently causing you stress.

• If your family is the interfering family or the one causing stress in your marriage, without condemning your family, you need to listen to your partner's feelings and provide support for them.

• Recognize that your unity with your partner has priority over every other relationship.

C. Together, come up with healthy boundaries that will put your marriage first.

Remember, to cultivate your marriage and grow together, you both must agree upon decisions about your money, time, and how information about your marriage is shared.

MAKE NOTES:

> "Boundaries protect the things that are of value to you. They keep you in alignment with what you have decided you want in life. That means the key to good boundaries is knowing what you want."
> —Adelyn Birch

Tips for Navigating Relationships with Extended Family

1. At the root of some of the issues with in-laws is competition, where the parents/family may feel like they must compete with their child's partner for attention, support, etc. You can reassure your in-laws by showing that you want to collaborate with them rather than compete.

   Collaboration may look like:

- calling to check on them at set times

- if you're in their home, being of use

- including them, within reason, in your activities

- being generous to them with your resources where possible

- being considerate of their family traditions and finding compromise around them

2. If something needs to be said to an interfering family, ideally it should come from the child to his/her parent/ family, not from the in-law.

3. Always be courteous, kind, and respectful to your in-laws. Anything else will only create further problems.

4. Create and maintain healthy boundaries. Be clear with each other about what extended family can and cannot participate in.

5. Always maintain a united front with extended family. You mustn't give room for anyone to put a wedge between the two of you.

6. Evaluate together your cultural perspectives and the parenting styles that you were raised with. This will help you both to understand the child-parent dynamic you each have and how you can best navigate it.

Continued Activity

Set some time aside this week to continue discussions about any past or current impact of your extended families on your relationship.

Listen, empathize, and comfort one another.

Together come up with any healthy boundaries that may be required.

CHAPTER 6

MONEY MATTERS IN *Marriage*

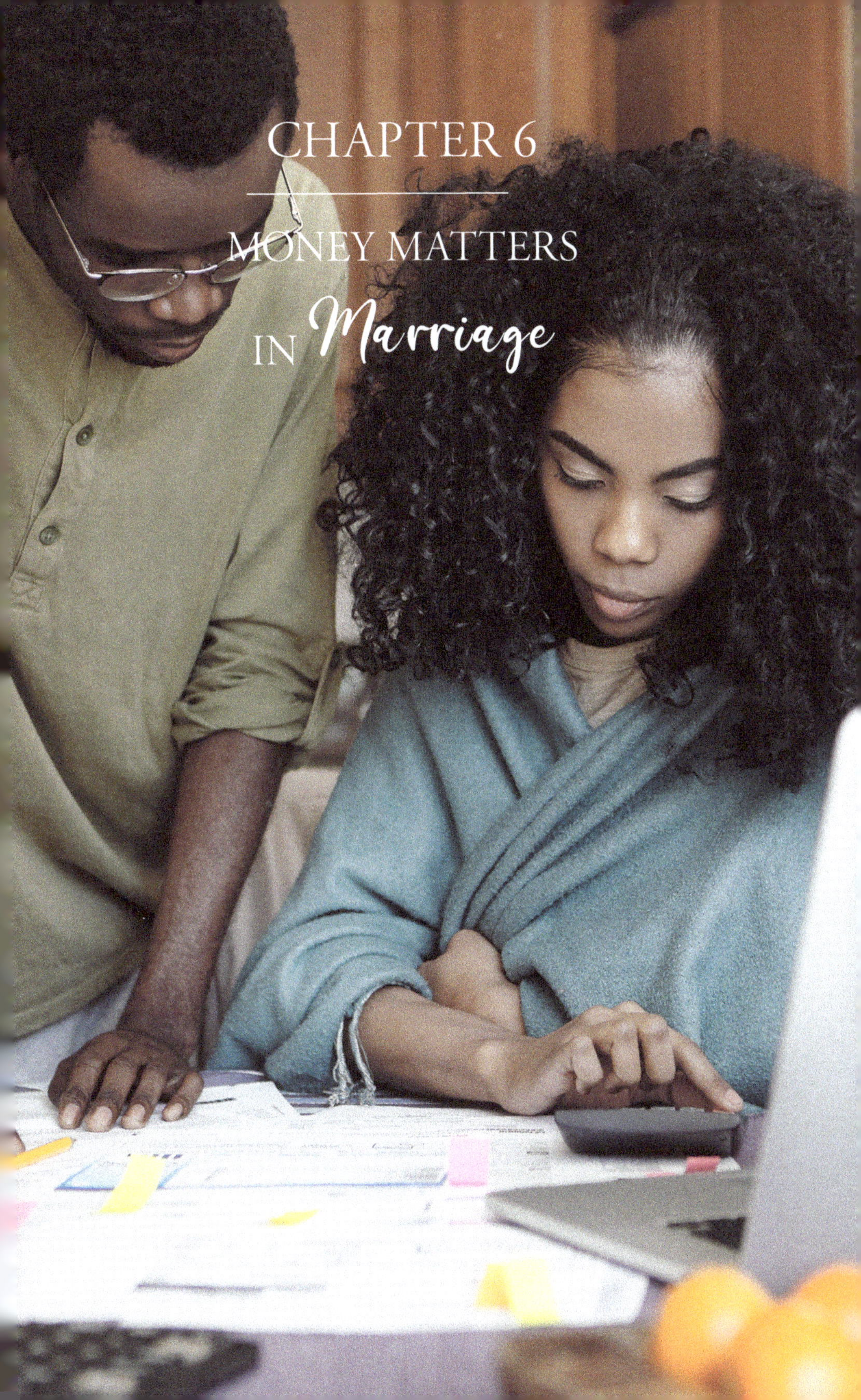

Your marriage relationship is your greatest asset; however, if you make your finances your greatest asset, that mindset will negatively impact your relationship.

There are four general ways in which married couples manage money:

1. There is the breadwinner/homemaker household, where only one partner works outside the home and the other partner works making the home. Often, the breadwinner will be the man, who may allocate a portion of his earnings for his wife to use for household expenses (breadwinner/homemaker). This dynamic is common in many Asian-African cultures.

2. Some couples have a "your money is your money, and my money is my money" arrangement; however, joint bills and financial responsibility will be divided between the couple (bill splitting).

3. Some couples have a "your money is your money, and my money is my money" arrangement; however, there is a commitment to putting a certain agreed percentage/amount of individual earnings into a joint account from where all joint financial commitments are met (quota allocation).

4. Some couples have a joint financial resources arrangement, where both their earnings go into a joint account from where all joint financial commitments are met, and all financial decisions are made together (joint accounting).

Activity 1   (5 minutes)

Individual Reflection

Reflect on the money management styles described above and think about the style you experienced with your parents or main caregiver.

How did this play out in your parents' or main caregiver's relationship?

MAKE NOTES:

Your beliefs and emotions about money are mostly shaped by your current or past life experiences as well as what was passed down by your parents.

Activity 2   (5 minutes)

Reflect on how money is currently managed in your relationship and evaluate if your style fits into any of the descriptions above.

From your experience to date with your partner, what are the advantages and disadvantages of your money management style?

Use the "Check Your Money Mindset" table to see if any apply to you.

MAKE NOTES:

Check Your Money Mindsets

Unhealthy Mindset	Healthy Mindset
Whoever makes more money in this relationship should control how all the money is spent.	We are united in our financial resources, savings, goals, and dreams.
My money is mine, and I don't have to be transparent about my earnings or savings.	We can be transparent about how much money we earn and spend, and what meaningful things we want to spend money on.
I contribute more financially to the relationship, so I'm more important or valuable to this relationship than my partner.	We are partners and we make collaborative decisions regardless of who makes more money.
We need to keep funding my partner's or extended family's addiction or unhealthy choices so that they won't leave or turn against me/us.	We're going to draw up a shared budget and get help for any unhealthy financial habits.

"Marriage is a partnership, and couples can't win with money unless they budget as a team."
—Dave Ramsey

Five Financial Principles in a Healthy Marriage

1. Recognize your different money personality.

Your money personality is likely different from your partner's. We would say it's highly probable that your money personalities will be opposites. One of you might be the saver, and the other is more inclined to spend, or one likes to work out the numbers, and the other partner would rather not be tied down by what the numbers say. It's important to recognize that these differences aren't necessarily a bad thing, and if managed well, they can be a great source of strength for your relationship.

Money mindsets are usually developed out of what researchers' term "money personality." Seven common money personalities have been identified. [19]

Activity 3 (20 minutes)

Individual Reflection

A. Read the sentences below. If the statement doesn't apply to you, put 0. If the statement sometimes applies to you, put 1. If the statement almost always applies to you, put 2.

No = 0   **Sometimes** = 1   **Almost Always** = 2

1. I know the exact cost of everything. ☐

2. If I pay in cash, I never ask for the change. ☐

3. The more money I make, the happier I feel. ☐

4. I enjoy going out with my friends without worrying about how much the outing costs. ☐

5. I have some debt that was from non-asset-related large purchase(s). ☐

6. I enjoy trying my luck. ☐

7. I'll take up extra work if I think I don't have enough money. ☐

8. I know exactly how much money I have in cash and my bank account ☐

9. I enjoy trendy things and showing them off. ☐

10. Only when I tidy my closet do I realize the number of unnecessary purchases I've made. ☐

11. I have a hard time resisting when offered something at a great price. ☐

12. I want to provide everything for my children. ☐

13. I don't like to throw out things that can still be used. ☐

14. I'm not sure we'll always be able to afford everything we need. ☐

15. I would rather make sandwiches than get food at a cafeteria. ☐

16. Occasionally I end up paying a few bills late. ☐

17. I have a few bad habits that have cost me a lot of money. ☐

18. I know how much money I have and want more of it. ☐

19. If I see something I like, I buy it. ☐

20. I tend to browse a lot before making a purchase. ☐

21. I like to buy people gifts so that they think better of me. ☐

22. I can save on expenses when I'm short of money. ☐

23. I'm puzzled about where my money goes. ☐

24. I don't enjoy cooking; I'd rather eat out. ☐

25. I love to save, and I don't necessarily need to have a goal for the money. ☐

26. Feels like bills are killing me. ☐

27. I'm in a desperate fix in debt. ☐

28. I would rather leave my money in the bank than put it in investments. ☐

29. I always make a shopping list. ☐

30. I love to reward myself with gifts. ☐

31. When I need more money, I take up extra work. ☐

32. I can ration my money. ☐

33. I believe that things will always work out and there is no need to worry about money. ☐

34. I often end up paying a few bills late. ☐

35. I keep track of all my expenses. ☐

Add up your scores in the table below. Where you score the highest is likely to be your predominant money personality; however, you can have a combination.

Questions	Total score	Money Personality
1, 8, 20, 25, 29		Compulsive Saver
2, 10, 21, 23, 30		Compulsive Spender
3, 9, 18, 24, 31		Compulsive Money Maker
4, 11, 19, 22, 32		Indifferent to Money
5, 13, 16, 26, 33		Saver-Spender
6, 12, 17, 27, 34		Gambler
7, 14, 15, 28, 35		Worrier

There are a total of 10 points available for each money personality you scored above.

The higher your score, the more likelihood that you are on the extreme of living out that money personality. Use the scale below to see where you currently fall (write your scores under the scale).

	0	5	10
	Low	Moderate	Extreme
Compulsive Saver			
Compulsive Spender			
Compulsive Money Maker			
Indifferent to Money			
Saver-Spender			
Gambler			
Worrier			

Use the picture on the next page to interpret your money personality.

The 7 Money Personality Types

The Compulsive Saver

- Saves money endlessly with no financial goal in mind
- Money represents security
- Very frugal and financially responsible
- Bargain-shopping expert
- May have a fear of irrational spending

The Compulsive Spender/Splurger

- Spends money on things not necessarily needed
- Spends when in emotional distress and for gratification
- Spontaneous spending on people, using their money to have others think more highly of them

The Free Spirit/ Saver-Spender

- Has traits between Savers and Spenders
- May start out saving but then give in to spending impulses
- Easygoing but lacks the needed discipline to secure their finance

The seven money personality types adapted from "Happy Money" by Ken Honda[1]

---

[1] https://www.simonandschuster.com/books/Happy-Money/Ken-Honda/9781501188374
Happy Money
The Japanese Art of Making Peace with Your Money, By Ken Honda
Japan's Bestselling Zen Millionaire

The Compulsive Money Maker

- Believes life is better when you earn more, money equals happiness
- Places high priority on growing wealth and making more money
- Gets pleasure from recognition for their wealth

The Money Monk/ Indifferent-to-Money

- Rarely thinks about money
- Feels that money should not influence the important decisions in life
- In extreme cases, this person believes that money is inherently bad or evil

The Gambler

- Has traits between Compulsive Money Makers and Spenser
- Takes big risks with money for the promise of reward and the pleasure that the reward could bring
- May gamble money away out of boredom

The Hoarder/Worrier

- Risk-averse and worries that money will run out
- May lack confidence in their ability to achieve financial freedom
- Worries about worst case scenario of what will happen if money runs out

Money Personalities Check-Up

Compulsive Saver: Celebrate your ability to manage money well and save. Reflect on how you can find a balance between saving and enjoying life. It may help to think about what your future goals are and how you can use your savings to achieve those goals.

Compulsive Spender: Celebrate the fact that you're very spontaneous and generous to people. Reflect on how you can develop a habit of making a budget plan and sticking to it.

Compulsive Money Maker: Celebrate your ability to make wealth. Reflect on how your relationships are faring and how you can prioritize relationships and making memories with your loved ones.

Indifferent to Money: Celebrate the fact that you don't need a lot of money to be happy. Reflect on how this may affect your partner and be mindful that you don't put all the financial responsibility on your partner. Make a point of knowing what your monthly expenses are and where your money is going.

Saver-Splurger: Celebrate your generous tendencies. Reflect on whether your financial habits need to be more disciplined and whether there's a need to plan a budget to organize your finances.

Gambler: Celebrate your ability to take risks. Reflect on the need to develop a strict saving habit and measure financial risks before taking them.

Worrier: Celebrate your ability to be cognizant of what could happen if you don't prepare financially for the future. Reflect on whether this is balanced or is turning into anxiety that is stealing your happiness.

Activity 3 (continued)

Individual Reflection

B. Make notes on your reflection about your money personality. Come up with ideas on how you can mediate any negative impact your money personality may be having on your relationship.

MAKE NOTES:

Five Financial Principles in a Healthy Marriage (continued)

2. **Keeping a joint bank account.**

Many couples believe that the best way to avoid money arguments in their relationship is to keep separate accounts and pay bills as allocated to them. This could be the groundwork for major problems in your marriage.

A scenario could be that you have decided to split the bills down the middle, or perhaps in a way you think is equitable. When the bills are covered, each of you can spend what you have left as you see fit. The reality is that over time, this scenario reduces the financial value of your marriage, impedes your ability to plan for long-term goals like buying a house or planning for retirement, and can build resentment. In the case of life outcomes where a partner loses their job, wants to go back to school to try a new career, needs to stay at home to raise children, or if there's any other situation where one partner may have to financially support the other, the lack of joint access to the finances could bring about discontentment and resentment. Bill splitting or quota allocation also gives room for financial infidelity.

According to the Chartered Professional Accountants of Canada, financial infidelity is a monetary act that violates a financial obligation or commitment established between you and your partner. It involves not being completely forthcoming with your partner about your finances regarding your spending, assets, investments, or debts. [20]

Another likely scenario is that one of you will earn more than the other partner. In a "your money, my money" dynamic, this could breed ground for salary difference being the source of contention. The person with more money may feel they have leverage over their partner or feel more entitled to the most say on big item purchases. On the other hand, in a "breadwinner/homemaker" dynamic, where the partner staying at home doesn't have equal access to the finances, it could be that the one staying at home feels or is made to feel like they don't have a say in the budgets or financial planning of the family. Unity in finances must be established and maintained in your relationship.

3. Discuss your financial choices and style.

You must have open communication about finances in your relationship. We have a compulsive saver married to the gambler/compulsive money maker dynamic in our relationship. This means one of us is perfectly happy to shop at Goodwill stores, and the other would prefer name-brand items. One of us will freely take financial risks that come with the promise of an increase, and the other would rather protect the amount saved without risking it. Some strategies for successful financial togetherness in the relationship include discussions about these financial preferences, evaluating our joint income and coming to a compromise on how much can be saved while still living life, buying some branded items on sale or at outlet malls and some items at Goodwill, and using a small portion of savings on financial investments seen as risks to the compulsive saver.

With awareness of your money personality, there must be respectful, open communication about financial preferences and compromise in how your joint finance can best serve your relationship, not just you as an individual.

4. Set financial expectations together.

Unmet and uncommunicated expectations about money can result in conflict. Set financial goals and expectations together. Be clear about financial goals you would like to work toward together, such as buying a house in a time frame, saving for a family holiday, or saving to start a family. Then put together a plan to make this happen. Use your financial personality differences to become a stronger, more united team.

5. **Keep all purchases in the open.**

Financial infidelity has been shown to occur in about one in four relationships [21] and is associated with low marital and life satisfaction for both partners, as well as linked to the occurrence of extramarital affairs. [21, 22] It is therefore important that spending be kept in the open to prevent falling into the trap of committing financial infidelity. Keeping a secret stash of money, making purchases that you keep in secret, or spending large sums on your credit cards all lead to a path of financial infidelity.

If you're guilty of having a side checking or savings account or secret credit card, now is the time to open up and own up. It's almost always better that truth comes out from the offender than it be found out by the one sinned against. You can work toward establishing financial trust again and recommit to the financial goals you set together.

Activity 4 (30 minutes)

Reflect on These Together

Show your partner your money personality and talk about how you can lend the strength from your financial personality to each other.

Reflect on the weaknesses of your financial personality and come up with strategies to mitigate these to grow and develop healthy habits.

A. Listen to how each other likes money to be used or managed.

B. Commit to handling your finances together, where the numbers person gently explains what the figures show, and the other partner listens and contributes positively. The saver recognizes the need of the spender, and the spender recognizes the need of the saver, and together you draw out a financial strategy for your relationship.

C. Think about how money is managed in your relationship right now and what changes you would like to make, if any.

D. What financial expectations would you like to set together?

MAKE NOTES:

If you recognize that there are deep issues, please seek the help of a counsellor, therapist, or financial adviser.

Continued Activity

Set some time aside this week to continue the conversation about your money personalities, past issues that may have resulted from your different money personalities, and future plans for managing your finances together.

CHAPTER 7

SEX IS A *Gift*

S ex in marriage is a gift to be enjoyed, not a gift to be left unwrapped, unexplored, or abused. It's a gift that has been shown to improve marital satisfaction, benefit your mental and physical health, [23] lower blood pressure, reduce stress, increase intimacy, and lower the divorce rate. [24]

Sex is the ultimate body language you can use to communicate to your partner that you love them, desire closeness with them, want protection or will protect them, want comfort, or will comfort them, and that you want a child together with them.

Healthy sexual relationships will:

- help you feel loved
- improve your bonding
- increase your tolerance
- deepen your relationship
- improve your emotional closeness
- increase your commitment to one another
- help you cope better with the pressures of life

"Sex should be the most rewarding when coupled with an affectionate connection to the partner."
—Anaïs Nin

Healthy sexual relationships can't happen without emotional connection, good communication, and mutual respect. The state of your sexual relationship can be a barometer of the health of your relationship. Not connecting emotionally, brutalizing one another emotionally or physically, being intellectually arrogant with your partner, or having unmanaged conflict in your relationship will impact the quality and frequency of your lovemaking. Your sexual intimacy will flow out of your emotional, intellectual, and spiritual intimacy. A block in one of these areas will create issues in one or more of the other areas.

Activity 1　(5 minutes)

Individual Reflection

What does sex mean to you?

MAKE NOTES:

> "Intimacy is totally a different dimension. It is allowing the other to come into you, to see you as you see yourself."
> —Osho

Understanding Your Partner's Sexual Attitudes

Sexual attitudes developed in the family of origin and within the community or society in which you grew up play a role in your sexual satisfaction now. Your sexual attitudes are your implicit beliefs and assumptions around sexual activity. [25] Children's sexual awareness begins early, and puberty is the major landmark in the development of sexuality. [26] Your exposure to correct information and educational material in your formative years will have a positive or negative influence on your sexual attitude.

In many reserved cultures, there is very little or no discussion about sexual matters with children, leaving the children to learn about sex from movies, other people, songs, the internet, and television. This has an impact on the perception of sexuality that is then developed.

Individuals whose experience growing up lacked attachment to a parent or had an unhealthy attachment to their parent(s), are likely to have inhibited sexual communication and poor sexual satisfaction. [25] If your experience involved healthy parental attachment, with an adequate amount of affection, closeness, and interdependence, you're more likely to enjoy closeness in your relationship, self-disclose your sexual needs, and be willing to encourage interdependence with your partner. [27]

Sex is ... perfectly natural. It's something that's pleasurable. It's enjoyable and it enhances a relationship. So why don't we learn as much as we can about it and become comfortable with ourselves as sexual human beings because we are all sexual?"
—Sue Johanson

Activity 2   (20 minutes)

Discuss the following with your partner:

A. What were your experiences growing up around sex? How did you learn to express sexuality?

B. Did you grow up with a balanced message about sex, or were the messages about sex-negative?

C. Think about how easy or not it is for you to talk about sex and sexual desires and share this with your partner. Does your upbringing make it easy or difficult for you?

"We're often afraid of being vulnerable, but vulnerability creates genuine connection."
—Gabby Bernstein

Factors That Foster Satisfying Sexual Experiences

1. Communication and Connection

2. Environment

3. Decision or Desire

1. Communication and Connection

Sex is a powerful way of connecting and bonding with someone you love. [28] It's important that you communicate with your partner which helps you to build a connection with them. The way we feel connected to another person is unique to us, and if we don't allow our partner to learn this, we can't get the sexual satisfaction we desire.

A healthy sex life is one of the greatest ways you can give validation to each other. This is also one of the greatest avenues to creating deep wounds and hurt. So, you must communicate about your sexual desires, and your dos and don'ts.

Sexual rejection without any communication could lead to various feelings, such as feeling:

• lonely

• rejected

• unloved

• undesirable

• unattractive

"Sex is always about emotions.
Good sex is about free emotions;
Bad sex is about blocked emotions."
—Deepak Chopra

Activity 3 (10 minutes)

A. Ask your partner, "How do you like to build a connection that will facilitate our sexual satisfaction and frequency?"

MAKE NOTES:

B. Ask your partner about their sexual likes and dislikes.

MAKE NOTES:

"Ultimately the bond of all companionship, whether in marriage or in friendship, is conversation."
—Oscar Wilde

2. Environment

You must create physical and emotional space that helps you both to relax into your lovemaking. This means that you should apply a bit of creativity to your sexual experience by:

- varying how and where you make love

- incorporating romance into your daily life

- varying who takes the initiative to initiate sex

- practicing non-sexual touch with your partner

- making an effort to keep fit and healthy for one another

- communicating about the variety of sexual experiences you would like to have and being sensitive to one another

"Good sex has to do with considering your partner first, not thinking of me first. When both people have this mindset, it revolutionizes lovemaking."
—Ife and Dami Adingupu

3. Decision or Desire

Sex is a decision. Sex is a desire. Whether decision came first, or desire came first is different for individuals. However, the decision to make love is what will give you the experience. Deciding that you want to make love to your partner means that you can now be intentional about having sex on your mind. This enables you to prepare your mind and plan what you will need to enjoy that sexual experience with your partner.

Studies on the neurophysiology of sexual arousal have shown that arousal is different for men and women. [29] For most people, especially women, the decision to have sex comes first and then arousal and desire come next. Generally, for men, the desire to have sex comes first, and then arousal and decision follow.

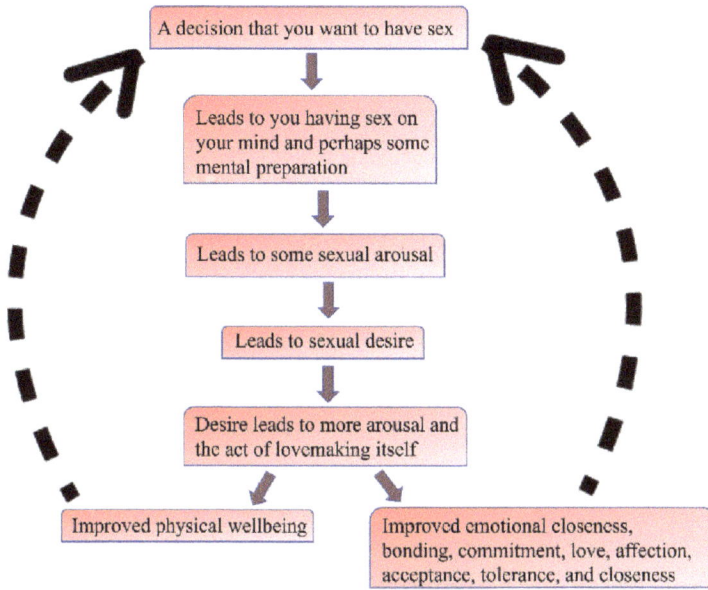

Decision first in the pathway to sexual experience

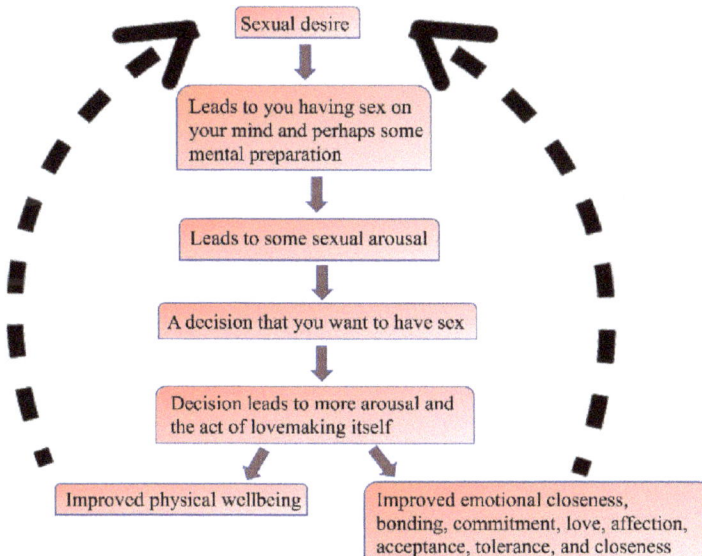

Desire first in the pathway to sexual experience.

Adapted from "The Female Sexual Response: A Different Model," by Basson, 2000 [29]

These pictures illustrate the relationship between sexual desire or decision and the emotional and health benefits.

Since sex is unlikely to be a neutral issue in your marriage, it's important to gain an understanding of what gets your partner in the mood for sex and then set up good communication, connection, and environment to facilitate this. If this isn't well managed in your relationship, the person with the higher libido or need for sex may reach out in vulnerability, and, if often rejected, that vulnerability may turn to feelings of frustration and anger.

"Sex will never be a neutral issue in your marriage. It will either draw you together or tear you apart."
—Dr. Juli Slattery

Activity 4: (20 minutes)

A. **Individual Reflection.**

Identify factors that may be affecting your sex life.

Some factors that may negatively impact your sex life are listed below.

Please select **Yes** if a statement applies to you, and **No** if it does not apply to you.

	Yes	No
I have had a previous negative sexual experience or sexual trauma.	☐	☐
I am currently feeling stressed and anxious about issues unrelated to our relationship.	☐	☐
I am currently dealing with body image issues.	☐	☐
I am currently dealing with other issues that cause me to feel shame.	☐	☐
I feel inadequate about my sexual performance.	☐	☐
There are unmanaged conflicts in our relationship.	☐	☐
There is a lack of emotional intimacy in our relationship.	☐	☐
There is a lack of non-sexual touch/intimacy in our relationship.	☐	☐

There is an unequal power dynamic in our relationship.	☐	☐
I believe that being turned on or having sexual desire is wrong.	☐	☐
I think my partner is thoughtless and would still want sex regardless of the circumstances, thereby making me feel used.	☐	☐
I can't talk freely to my partner about our lovemaking and my sexual needs.	☐	☐
There is an issue with pornography.	☐	☐
Other health issues inhibit me from wanting to have sex.	☐	☐

B. Use the sexual desire or decision pictures to identify your current pathway to sexual experience.

MAKE NOTES:

Share your answers to Activity 4A and 4B with your partner.

C. Talk about some of the factors that may be affecting your sex life using the "I statements."

D. Come up with ideas about creative changes that you could make individually or together to improve your sex life.

Be specific about the changes you want to make.

Examples:

I want to take the initiative to initiate sex more often.

I would like us to go somewhere else occasionally to have a different environment for a sexual experience.

You must seek to understand one another, empathize with each other, and offer support and encouragement where needed.

Make Notes:

"Sex is an emotion in motion."
—Mae West

Continued Activity

Marital satisfaction is a genuine feeling of pleasure, satisfaction, and joyfulness experienced by a husband and wife when they consider all aspects of their marriage. [30] This is severely affected by your sexual experience and the satisfaction you get from your sexual relationship with your partner.

This week, think of small actions that you can take to enhance your marital satisfaction, or think of things that you can stop doing that will enhance your marital satisfaction.

Examples:

I will intentionally put away my phone for 30 minutes and spend that time talking to my partner about my day.

I will be intentional about being respectful to my partner in all our exchanges.

I will plan a fun activity that we can do together.

I will do something romantic for my partner.

See the next page for ideas for conversation starters.

MAKE NOTES:

"What will seduce a person is the effort we expend on their behalf, showing how much we care, how much they are worth. Leaving things to chance is a recipe for disaster and reveals that we do not take love and romance very seriously."
—Robert Greene

Twenty Questions to Enhancing Sexual Intimacy

1. What turns you on?

2. What do you consider to be foreplay?

3. How would you like for us to initiate sex?

4. What does a great sex life look like for you?

5. What would have sex more romantic and passionate for you?

6. Do you currently feel rejected sexually by me? How can we handle this?

7. Does it ever feel to you like any form of touch from me is a request for sex?

8. How can I help you to feel safer with me during sexual intimacy?

9. Is there anything you would like to try sexually that we haven't yet?

10. How would you like to communicate that you're in the mood for sex?

11. Do you like to have music or candles to set a romantic atmosphere for sex?

12. Do you think we have a difference in our sexual desire? How can we handle this?

13. Are there things that I do or say that make you feel bad about your body and put you off sex?

14. Do you ever feel pressured by me to have sex, even when you don't feel like it? How can we handle this?

15. How can I communicate to you that I'm not in the mood for sex, without it feeling like a rejection?

16. Are there any parts of foreplay that you like the least? What would you like me to do differently?

17. During sexual intimacy, are there parts of your body you would like me to focus more attention on?

18. Are there things that I do that make you feel good and encourage you to want to have sex with me?

19. Have you ever watched pornography? If yes, how is this affecting you? Or how has it affected you?

20. Are there things I do or say about your body that make you feel good about your body? Is there anything else that I could do?

CHAPTER 8

Love OUT LOUD

L ove is more than what we feel; it's *what* we do or say, *how* we do or say it, and *when* we do or say it. The way you receive love and express love is not likely to be the same; however, many of us would default to expressing love in the way we prefer to receive it.

Loving your partner well is an art that can be mastered, and as seasons change, it's an art that must be fine-tuned and polished. This is because the way we each feel and receive love is unique to us, shaped by our experiences, personalities, and peculiarities.

Learning how your partner receives love provides an opportunity for you to develop a closer relationship and you can use that knowledge to grow a healthy relationship. Love expressed well always costs you something. Often, the cost is your time, emotions, and vulnerability.

Five love languages have been identified, and research shows that we each have a dominant one. [31]

The five love languages are:

1. Quality Time

2. Gifts or Thoughtful Presents

3. Acts of Service or Kind Actions

4. Physical Touch or Physical Affection

5. Words of Affirmation or Loving Words

One of these love languages will communicate love more effectively than the others to each one of us. It's important that you recognize how your partner receives love and then love them in that manner.

1. Quality Time

This love language focuses on a person's desire to experience togetherness and connectedness, and it requires your undivided attention. For a person with this love language, it's important that their partner sets time apart for them and is intentional about what they do together during this time.

Intentional eye contact tells a partner with this love language that they have your full attention, you see them, and that you are interested and committed to spending that time with them. The more time you spend together with your partner engaged in activities and positive communication, the closer you'll become and the greater your relationship satisfaction. [32]

Regardless of what your love language is, quality time is necessary for you to strengthen your relationship and form a deeper bond.

Quality time is important because it:

- builds memories
- improves intimacy
- keeps you connected
- helps keep the romance alive
- improves relationship self-esteem
- builds closeness and commitment
- provides an opportunity for meaningful communication
- provides an opportunity to have fun and laugh together

"The best gift you can give anyone is to spend quality time with them."
—Laurence Overmire

Activity 1A (10 minutes)

Reflect on these together.

- When you were dating, can you recall how many hours you spent talking to each other per week?

MAKE NOTES:

- Can you recall how many dates you went on per month when you were dating?

MAKE NOTES:

- Estimate how many hours you spend talking to each other now per week.

MAKE NOTES:

- How many dates would you say you have per month now?

  (A date can simply be a time you set up to spend quality time together without any distractions or other people's interactions).

MAKE NOTES:

Activity 1B (5 minutes)

Individual reflection:

- Write down the things that you like to do for fun.

Make Notes:

- Review your list of things you like to do and identify which ones you would like to share with your partner.

Make Notes:

- Now you have some ideas of things you can do together, and your partner can come and be a part of them and vice versa.

Activity 1C (10 minutes)

Thinking Forward Together

Show each other your lists and identify which activities you could do together.

Together, decide how many dates per month you'd like to plan for and commit to prioritizing and protecting that time from any other life pressure that will bid for that set time.

MAKE NOTES:

Continued Activity

This week, set a time to synchronize your diaries and find a date over the next month for a date night.

Discuss with your partner what you'd like to do for your date night that will be:

- enjoyable for both of you
- within an agreed budget

Tips for Spending Quality Time Together

A. Connect with conversation: Meaningful conversation involves two people sharing their feelings, thoughts, ideas, desires, fears, hopes, and dreams. Spend your time together learning about each other, taking turns to listen and ask open-ended questions.

Use "why," "how," and "what" to start your sentence to show your curiosity and interest in getting to know your spouse or keeping up to date with what's going on in their life. Avoid topics that you're currently having conflict about. Your set time for quality time is not the time to deal with conflict; it's a time to connect and enjoy each other.

Examples

- Why do you think … happened like that?
- How did that … make you feel?
- What was that … like for you?

B. Create a positive atmosphere: Using eye contact, smiles, nods, and physical touch appropriately during this time will help you feel closer to each other.

C. Pay attention to the small daily moments. You don't need to wait until a set date night to have quality time. Doing daily chores together, going for a walk, or going to bed at the same time are ways you can be present in the moment to have quality time together.

D. Plan play time: Find out what you each like to do for fun and take turns planning those activities and enjoying them together.

E. Unplug from technology. In our culture today, technology has become almost essential to daily living; however, it has also come with the disadvantage known as "phubbing" in many relationships. Phubbing is defined as the act of ignoring someone you're with and giving attention to your mobile device instead. [33]

2. Gifts or Thoughtful Presents

If receiving gifts is your partner's primary love language, every little and big thoughtful gift you give tells them that you have them on your mind. Each time they see this gift, they're reminded that they are loved. It's not about the cost of the gift you give but the thought, sentiment, and intentionality you put into the gift.

Some examples of how to speak this love language include:

- picking wildflowers and presenting them to them

- leaving nice notes in places they will find it

- making them breakfast and bringing it to them in bed

- bringing them a small "just because I love you" gift

- having their favourite food/drink/treat delivered to them at work

- sending them a link to a romantic song that reminded you of them

- buying your partner's favourite snack when you're at the store and presenting it to them

- making special occasions, like their birthday, a big deal and an opportunity to dote on them

- taking them on a date that includes all the things they like (restaurant/food, activity, movie, etc.)

- being present for the important things or events they ask you to be there for. Your time dedicated to them is a precious gift.

Activity 2 (10 minutes)

Reflect on this together.

Think about a memorable gift that your partner gave you and tell them why it's memorable for you.

3. Acts of Service and Kind Actions in Motion

This love language requires you to serve your partner with intentionality, performing kind, helpful, and thoughtful deeds without them having to ask you. For this to be meaningful, it should have an element of you taking initiative and perhaps going out of your way to do a kind, thoughtful deed. This entails you paying careful attention to the small details of your life together and creating a safe space for your partner to ask when they do need you to do something for them.

Kind actions are very impactful for the partner that receives love with this love language because it will make them feel loved, taken care of, seen, safe, and like they can trust you to have their back with the small and big things. The bonus for the person serving in this way is that you're showing relational leadership by doing acts of service because the mark of a true leader is serving others before serving themselves. Your selfless acts will inspire your partner and others in your home to aspire to do the same.

Some Acts of Service to Consider

- Take the trash out.
- Put the toilet seat down.
- Offer a back and/or foot rub.
- Run a bath for your partner.
- Get their car washed and fill up the gas.
- Offer to run some of their errands for them.
- Take care of some household organizing and planning.
- Offer to give your partner a day off from house chores while you do the chores.

Activity 3A (15 minutes)

Pay attention to the small details of your life together to get ideas of acts of service you can do.

Reflect on this individually.

Ask yourself:

- What chores does my partner hate doing but must do?
- What household chores can I take on to relieve my partner?
- How does my partner like their tea/coffee or any beverage?
- What strengths and/or skills do I have that I can use to serve my partner in their profession?
- What task(s) has my partner asked me to do that I've put off doing for some time?
- What random kind deeds can I do for my partner?

MAKE NOTES:

Activity 3B (10 minutes)

Reflect on this together.

Ask each other, "What deeds can I do that will be meaningful for you and make you feel loved?"

MAKE NOTES:

4. Physical Touch or Physical Affection

A person with physical touch as their love language expresses and receives affection through touch (non-sexual and sexual), physical closeness, and other forms of physical connection. Kissing, hugging, holding hands, shoulder touch, and sex are all ways of showing love through this love language. If your partner's primary love language is touch, congratulations! This is a gift that you give, and it gives back to you at the same time, if you speak it well.

Touch affects the person being touched and the one doing the touching. Touch causes the brain to release the bonding hormone oxytocin and feel-good hormones like dopamine and serotonin, and it decreases your stress levels by reducing the amount of stress hormones, like cortisol and norepinephrine, that your body produces.[34]

Touch is the first sense and language we learn as a child. This means that your childhood, culture, and life experiences have a great influence on this love language and your ability to give and receive it. Your partner's and your comfort level with touch may therefore be different. If this is the case, don't despair. Touch is a language that can be learned.

By creating a positive atmosphere in your relationship, resolving conflict, having open conversations, and starting with small actions like sitting close to each other and holding hands, you will develop the language of touch.

Advantages of Positive Touch

- Makes your partner feel safe
- Strengthens your relationship
- Fosters and enhances cooperation
- Increases the sense of connectivity with your partner

Activity 4   (20 minutes)

Do this together.

Reflect on whether physical touch or physical affection is used to the extent that you would like in your relationship and discuss it with your partner.

Identify if there are issues that are impeding the expression of this love language and discuss them with your partner.

MAKE NOTES:

5. Words of Affirmation and Loving Words

Words of affirmation communicate to your spouse that you love, appreciate, and respect them. This doesn't only have to be in spoken words; it could be in written form too. Words of affirmation can't just be in your thoughts. They need to be spoken or written to your partner.

If your partner's primary love language is words of affirmation, using this effectively will help them to feel appreciated and loved. It will increase their level of satisfaction in your marriage and their sense of self-worth and motivation. This not only benefits your partner, but research shows that using kind words and giving compliments also increases the giver's well-being.[35] So you stand to gain a lot too by using loving words freely and sincerely.

Refusing to use words at all or using your words to criticize or tear down your partner, will set your relationship on a path of destruction. Words can create a mental image in your partner's mind, so you must decide what image you want them to have from the words spoken by you.

Tips for Using Words of Affirmation Well

Your words must be:

- genuine
- specific
- present in the moment
- unique to your partner
- positive, focusing on what is good

Examples:

I'm sorry that I …

You inspire me to …

I am so thankful for you.

I believe in you; you've got this.

That dress/shirt looks great on you.

I couldn't have done … without you

Things feel better when you're here.

I'm so happy we're doing life together.

I love how you love me, care for me, look at me …

I see that you're hurting/stressed. How can I help you?

I really respected the strength you showed in that situation.

Thank you for (insert specifics, focusing on what is good).

When you supported/helped me with … it made me feel loved.

I loved the time we spent together doing … I'd love to do that with you again soon.

"Kind words do not cost much. Yet they accomplish much."

Blaise Pascal

Activity 5 (20 minutes)

Ask each other:

A. "What can I say to you that feels romantic to you?"

MAKE NOTES:

B. "What words should I never say to you, even in playfulness?"

MAKE NOTES:

C. Ask each other, "What do I say that feels unloving to you?"

There are obvious words that you know are unloving, so if these words have been used against one another in the past, this is an opportunity to acknowledge that and ask for forgiveness. There are also times that you may have said things unknowingly that caused hurt to your partner. This activity will help you identify these.

MAKE NOTES:

D. You may already know your love language or not. As season changes in your life and your relationship, sometimes your primary love language may also change. Activity 6 will serve as a check-up for which love language may be your primary love language currently.

Activity 6 (20 minutes)

A. Identify Your Love Language

For each statement below, think about how they apply to you.

In the box, put the number that corresponds to the statement that applies to you almost always, sometimes, or never.

Never = 0   **Sometimes** = 1   **Almost Always** = 2

	Almost Always	Sometimes	Never
1. I feel cared for and loved when my partner offers to take care of the house chores and give me the day off.	☐	☐	☐
2. I like being with others, especially my partner, more than being alone.	☐	☐	☐
3. I get a thrill when my partner expresses gratitude toward me.	☐	☐	☐
4. Receiving spontaneous kisses (on the lips, forehead, cheeks, or elsewhere) makes me feel loved.	☐	☐	☐

5. When I am stressed, I feel instantly calmed or relaxed when my partner puts their hand on mine or rubs my shoulders.

☐ ☐ ☐

6. Unexpected praise from my partner for something I did makes me feel loved.

☐ ☐ ☐

7. When my partner anticipates my needs and meets these needs, it makes me feel loved.

☐ ☐ ☐

8. Postponed activities or dates with my partner upsets me greatly.

☐ ☐ ☐

9. I feel loved when my partner brings me back something from a business trip or the gas station.

☐ ☐ ☐

10. It upsets me a great deal if my partner forgets to get me a present on birthdays, anniversaries, and other gift-giving holidays.

☐ ☐ ☐

11. It feels strange to be sitting next to my partner and not be touching in some way.

☐ ☐ ☐

12. It's more important to me that my partner shows me they love me through what they do rather than what they say.

☐ ☐ ☐

13. I prefer to do most activities with my partner or others than to do it by myself.

☐ ☐ ☐

14. I love to find spontaneous romantic notes left for me by my partner.

☐ ☐ ☐

15. Little physical gestures like holding hands and resting my head on my partner's shoulder are some of my favourite things about being in a relationship.

☐ ☐ ☐

16. I enjoy listening to others and giving them my undivided attention.

☐ ☐ ☐

17. If my partner fails to do something they promised they'd do, it makes me very upset.

☐ ☐ ☐

18. My partner doesn't need to say "I love you" a bunch for me to feel loved. I can feel it through the way they hold or kiss me.

☐ ☐ ☐

19. My partner telling me they appreciate having me in their life makes me love them more.

☐ ☐ ☐

20. If my partner does little things for me, it means a great deal to me. ☐ ☐ ☐

21. I always make time for my loved ones, even if I'm not physically with them. ☐ ☐ ☐

22. I love to receive a compliment. ☐ ☐ ☐

23. Receiving a long, warm hug from my partner makes me feel like they really care about me. ☐ ☐ ☐

24. I treasure anything my partner gives me that they put some thought into. ☐ ☐ ☐

25. I enjoy having new experiences with my partner more than receiving physical gifts. ☐ ☐ ☐

26. When my partner remembers something that I mentioned I wanted ages ago and gets it for me, I feel incredibly seen and loved. ☐ ☐ ☐

27. I value any support from my partner, especially when they offer to take care of day-to-day duties. ☐ ☐ ☐

28. When my partner doesn't touch me in a group setting, I notice it and it upsets me. ☐ ☐ ☐

29. When my partner encourages me, it makes me feel very much loved. ☐ ☐ ☐

30. I feel lonely when I haven't spent enough time with my partner. ☐ ☐ ☐

31. "Just because" gifts from my partner make me feel loved. ☐ ☐ ☐

32. When my partner does home projects for me, it makes me feel loved. ☐ ☐ ☐

33. I cherish surprises, as they make me feel loved. ☐ ☐ ☐

34. I need my partner to tell me they care about me often. ☐ ☐ ☐

35. I love the process of giving sweet, romantic presents to my partner. ☐ ☐ ☐

Love Language Check

Add up your total score. The love language with the highest score is likely to be your primary love language.

Love language	Statement number	Total score
Quality Time	2, 8, 13, 16, 21, 25, 30	
Thoughtful Presents	9, 10, 24, 26, 31, 33, 35	
Acts of Service	1, 7, 12, 17, 20, 27, 32	
Physical Touch	4, 5, 11, 15, 18, 23, 28	
Words of Affirmation	3, 6, 14, 19, 22, 29, 34	

Love language	Statements	Total score
Quality Time	2, 8, 13, 16, 21, 25, 30	
Thoughtful Presents	9, 10, 24, 26, 31, 33, 35	
Acts of Service	1, 7, 12, 17, 20, 27, 32	
Physical Touch	4, 5, 11, 15, 18, 23, 28	
Words of Affirmation	3, 6, 14, 19, 22, 29, 34	

To confirm these results, we encourage you to use Dr. Gary Chapman's love languages quiz, referenced in the footnote. 2

---

2   https://5lovelanguages.com/quizzes/love-language
Reference to the Five Love Languages is from the best-selling book, *The 5 Love Languages* ®: *The Secret to Love that Lasts* by Dr. Gary Chapman'. Used with permission.

Word of Caution on the Love Languages

Knowing exactly how your partner receives love is a powerful tool in your hand. You can use this knowledge for immense good or evil in your relationship. Be very careful that this knowledge is only used to build your relationship and not to intentionally withhold love, thereby hurting your partner and your marriage.

"Knowledge is power. Power to do good ... or to do evil. Be careful with what you do with the knowledge that you gain."

—Ife and Dami Adingupu

Moving Forward from Here

Many relationships are falling apart, some because of hideous experiences like infidelity, domestic abuse, and/or addictions that a partner refuses to treat. However, many are because of a cumulation of many small behaviors that come from individuals not being well prepared to be a good partner, due to their past experiences or not paying attention to the needs of their partner.

Many of your behaviors are guided by experiences you had in your home of origin, or in past relationships that left you broken and hurt. When you refuse to **acknowledge** the brokenness and hurt from your past, there's a high likelihood that the same hidden, unacknowledged brokenness will result in internal disputes or voices that will make your relationship vulnerable to attacks from you.

Acknowledging that the brokenness and hurt from your life's experiences exist is essential. This needs to be followed by an **awareness** of how this plays out in your relationship. With awareness and understanding must come **action**.

You can act by getting help and healing for hurt and brokenness from mentors, relationship coaches, or trained counsellors. You must acknowledge your experiences, become aware of how these experiences may be playing out in your marriage/relationship, and act to take positive steps that will mitigate the negative impacts of those past experiences on your current relationship.

Throughout this book, you've had opportunities to acknowledge areas that may need working on or healing, gain understanding through deeper awareness of yourself and your relationship and engage in activities that will enable you to act in ways that will grow a thriving relationship.

This book serves as a guide to how you can transform from a broken background to a healthy relationship. The extensive bulk of the journey now depends on you deciding to take steps daily and consistently doing things in and for your relationship that will turn your trials and traumas into a testament to your growth. Your hardships can be your teacher for the future you want.

We do recognize that some marriages with patterns of destruction may not be sustainable or safe to continue in. If you think this is your current experience, please use Appendix 3 to check the common red flags. Should any of these red flags be present in your marriage, please speak to a trusted friend, mentor, elder, coach, spiritual leader, or counsellor as soon as possible.

"A deep sense of love and belonging is an incredible need of all men, women, and children. We are biologically, cognitively, physically, and spiritually wired to love, to be loved, and to belong"
—Brené Brown

APPENDIX 1

Positive emotions

Awe

Assured

Affirmed

Confident

Carefree

Encouraged

Forgiven

Glad

Hopeful

Liberated

Positive

Respected

Secure

Sure

Trusting

Worthwhile

Appreciated

Affection

Calm

Comforted

Delighted

Ecstatic

Free

Happy

Interested

Loved

Relaxed

Relieved

Serene

Supported

Understood

Amazed

Accepted

Content

Capable

Determined

Excited

Grateful

Humbled

Joyful

Peaceful

Remorseful

Safe

Satisfied

Thrilled

Valuable

Negative emotions

Abandoned	Afraid	Angry
Annoyed	Anxious	Apathetic
Ashamed	Apologetic	Bored
Confused	Cross	Defeated
Depressed	Disappointed	Disgusted
Disrespected	Dissatisfied	Embarrassed
Exposed	Frustrated	Grieved
Guilty	Humiliated	Hurt
Inadequate	Insecure	Insignificant
Irritated	Jealous	Loathsome
Lonely	Miserable	Misunderstood
Nervous	Numb	Overwhelmed
Pressured	Rage	Resentful
Rejected	Sad	Scared
Sorrowful	Scorn	Terrified
Unappreciated	Unloved	Upset
Used	Useless	Vulnerable

APPENDIX 2

Thirty Ideas to Communicate Your Needs

1. I need you to tell me that I'm sexy.

2. I need you to do more housework.

3. I need to have more respect from you.

4. I need for us to have adventures together.

5. I need you to support me with your family.

6. I need for us to have a plan for our savings.

7. I need to hear more compliments from you.

8. I need you to be more affectionate with me.

9. I want us to talk about how we have changed.

10. I need to hear you say "I love you" more often.

11. I need you to show interest in how my day went.

12. I need you to touch me affectionately more often.

13. I need us to have more arts and/or music in our life.

14. I need to hear from you that we are still best friends.

15. I need to have some alone time for myself sometimes.

16. I need to get dressed up and go out to have fun with you.

17. I need you to plan some fun activities for us to do together.

18. I need to hear from you that you find my intellect attractive.

19. I need you to show more interest in me and ask me more questions.

20. I need you to talk to me and not shut me out, even when we disagree.

21. When I'm feeling low, I need you to listen and empathize with me.

22. I need you to put down your phone or focus on me from your computer when I want to talk to you.

23. I need you to offer to do the household chores sometimes so I can get some relief.

24. I need for us to have a better balance between our work and family life.

25. I need us to pursue having a closer relationship with our extended family.

26. I need us to have weekends where we do activities together as a family.

27. I need you to speak calmly to me when you're upset, without yelling at me.

28. I need you to listen more to me and not try to give advice or solve the issue.

29. I need to hear from you that you appreciate the effort I put into keeping our home, and the long hours and hard work to provide for us.

30. I need us to set health goals and support each other in achieving them.

APPENDIX 3

RED FLAGS

Some red flags that may indicate you are in a destructive marriage/relationship.

- You feel scared for yourself. This could be due to either your physical or emotional safety being threatened.

- You feel controlled by your partner. There are many instances that you can identify where you're not allowed to make your own choices or decisions.

- There is a consistent element of confusion, where you're made to feel confused about decisions or agreements that were made, but your partner denies ever agreeing to such.

- You are regularly devalued with words and made to feel like your feelings, goals, opinions, and needs don't matter.

- You regularly feel that your partner is deceiving you, or you have evidence that your partner is deceitful.

- You're being isolated by your partner. They will object to you going to see friends and/or family and even refuse to meet your friends and/or family. They may cast aspersions on you if you decide to have a relationship with those friends/ family anyway.

- You feel like you're losing your sanity because of your marriage/ relationship experience, and your partner doesn't seem willing to change the behavior that is contributing to this feeling.

If you would like to explore marriage or relationship coaching, contact us at **www.thrivingrelationshipsnow.com**
To purchase the video series that complements this guide, visit **www.thrivingrelationshipsnow.com**

Follow us on social media.

IG: @adinxfam_themarriageadvocates

TikTok: @TheMarriageAdvocates

YouTube: @themarriageadvocates5

REFERENCES

1. Vaish A, Grossmann T, and Woodward A. Not all emotions are created equal: the negativity bias in social-emotional development. *Psychol Bull* 2008; 134: 383-403. 2008/05/01. DOI: 10.1037/0033-2909.134.3.383.

2. Woolley K and Fishbach A. Motivating Personal Growth by Seeking Discomfort. *Psychological Science* 2022; 33: 510-523. DOI: 10.1177/09567976211044685.

3. Reissman C, Aron A and Bergen MR. Shared Activities and Marital Satisfaction: Causal Direction and Self-Expansion versus Boredom. *Journal of Social and Personal Relationships* 1993; 10: 243-254. DOI: 10.1177/026540759301000205.

4. Aron A, Norman CC, Aron EN, et al. Couples shared participation in novel and arousing activities and experienced relationship quality. *J Pers Soc Psychol* 2000; 78: 273-284. 2000/03/09. DOI: 10.1037//0022-3514.78.2.273.

5. Maloney ME and Moore P. From aggressive to assertive(). *Int J Womens Dermatol* 2020; 6: 46-49. 2020/02/12. DOI: 10.1016/j.ijwd.2019.09.006.

6. Zimmerman A. The Four Levels Of Communication, https://www.drzimmerman.com/tuesdaytip/interpersonal-communications-have-four-levels-and-all-require-communication-skills-to-properly-manage?doing_wp_cron=1682687889.8138999938964843750000 (2016, accessed 28th April 2023).

7. Dictionary.com. Dictionary. 2023.

8. Putman D. The Emotions of Courage. *Journal of Social Philosophy* 2001; 32: 463-470. DOI: https://doi.org/10.1111/0047-2786.00107.

9. Merriam-Webster. Silent treatment. In: Dictionary M-Wc, (ed.). 2023.

10.   Manes S. Making Sure Emotional Flooding Doesn't Capsize Your Relationship, https://www.gottman.com/blog/making-sure-emotional-flooding-doesnt-capsize-your-relationship/ (2013, accessed 18th May 2023 2023).

11.   Wohl MJA and McGrath AL. The Perception of Time Heals All Wounds: Temporal Distance Affects Willingness to Forgive Following an Interpersonal Transgression. *Personality and Social Psychology Bulletin* 2007; 33: 1023-1035. DOI: 10.1177/0146167207301021.

12.   Worthington EL, Jr., Witvliet CV, Pietrini P, et al. Forgiveness, health, and well-being: a review of evidence for emotional versus decisional forgiveness, dispositional forgivingness, and reduced unforgiveness. *J Behav Med* 2007; 30: 291-302. 2007/04/25. DOI: 10.1007/s10865-007-9105-8.

13.   Association AP. Forgiveness, https://dictionary.apa.org/forgiveness (2023, accessed 29th April 2033).

14.   Lawler KA, Younger JW, Piferi RL, et al. A change of heart: cardiovascular correlates of forgiveness in response to interpersonal conflict. *J Behav Med* 2003; 26: 373-393. 2003/11/05. DOI: 10.1023/a:1025771716686.

15.   Witvliet CvO, Ludwig TE and Laan KLV. Granting forgiveness or harboring grudges: Implications for emotion, physiology, and health. *Psychological science* 2001; 12: 117-123.

16.   Worthington EL, vanOyen Witvliet C, Lerner AJ, et al. Forgiveness in Health Research and Medical Practice. *EXPLORE* 2005; 1: 169-176. DOI: https://doi.org/10.1016/j.explore.2005.02.012.

17.   Aron A, Aron, E. N., & Smollan, D. . Inclusion of Other in the Self Scale and the structure of interpersonal closeness. . *Journal of Personality and Social Psychology* 1992; 63: 596–612.

18.   Morris AS, Silk JS, Steinberg L, et al. The Role of the Family Context in the Development of Emotion Regulation. *Soc Dev* 2007; 16: 361-388. 2007/05/01. DOI: 10.1111/j.1467-9507.2007.00389.x.

19. Alexandra L, Erzsebet N and Boglarka Z. FINANCIAL PERSONALITY TYPES AND ATTITUDES THAT AFFECT FINANCIAL INDEBTEDNESS. *International Journal of Social Science and Economic Research,* 2017; 2: 4687-4704.

20. Jones SN. Know the warning signs when sniffing out financial infidelity, https://www.cpacanada.ca/en/news/canada/2020-11-16-financial-infidelity (2020, accessed 31st January 2023).

21. Jeanfreau M, Noguchi K, Mong MD, et al. Financial Infidelity in Couple Relationships. *Journal of Financial Therapy* 2018; 9. DOI: https://doi.org/10.4148/1944-9771.1159.

22. Dew JP, Saxey MT and Mettmann A. Money lies and extramarital ties: Predicting separate and joint occurrences of financial deception and extramarital infidelity. *Front Psychol* 2022; 13: 1038169. 2022/12/10. DOI: 10.3389/fpsyg.2022.1038169.

23. Zhang Y and Liu H. A National Longitudinal Study of Partnered Sex, Relationship Quality, and Mental Health Among Older Adults. *J Gerontol B Psychol Sci Soc Sci* 2020; 75: 1772-1782. 2019/05/28. DOI: 10.1093/geronb/gbz074.

24. Debrot A, Meuwly N, Muise A, et al. More Than Just Sex: Affection Mediates the Association Between Sexual Activity and Well-Being. *Pers Soc Psychol Bull* 2017; 43: 287-299. 2017/09/15. DOI: 10.1177/0146167216684124.

25. Bryant C. *The Development of Sexual Attitudes in the Family of Origin and Sexual Satisfaction Later in Life.* University of Nevada, Las Vegas, 2016.

26. Kar SK, Choudhury A and Singh AP. Understanding normal development of adolescent sexuality: A bumpy ride. *J Hum Reprod Sci* 2015; 8: 70-74. 2015/07/15. DOI: 10.4103/0974-1208.158594.

27. Strait JG, Sandberg JG, Larson JH, et al. The relationship between family-of-origin experiences and sexual satisfaction in married couples. *Journal of Family Therapy* 2015; 37: 361-385. DOI: 10.1111/1467-6427.12007.

28. Weiner-Davis M. The sex-starved marriage. *TEDxCU*. 2014.

29. Basson R. The Female Sexual Response: A Different Model. *Journal of Sex & Marital Therapy* 2000; 26: 51-65. DOI: 10.1080/009262300278641.

30. Ziaee T, Jannati Y, Mobasheri E, et al. The Relationship between Marital and Sexual Satisfaction among Married Women Employees at Golestan University of Medical Sciences, Iran. *Iran J Psychiatry Behav Sci* 2014; 8: 44-51. 2014/07/24.

31. Chapman GD. *The Five Love Languages.* . MI: Farmington Hills, 2010.

32. Hogan JN, Crenshaw AO, Baucom KJW, et al. Time Spent Together in Intimate Relationships: Implications for Relationship Functioning. *Contemp Fam Ther* 2021; 43: 226-233. 2021/08/03. DOI: 10.1007/s10591-020-09562-6.

33. Dictionary C. Phubbing. UK: Cambridge University Press & Assessment, 2023.

34. Ellingsen DM, Leknes S, Løseth G, et al. The Neurobiology Shaping Affective Touch: Expectation, Motivation, and Meaning in the Multisensory Context. *Front Psychol* 2015; 6: 1986. 2016/01/19. DOI: 10.3389/fpsyg.2015.01986.

35. Boothby EJ and Bohns VK. Why a Simple Act of Kindness Is Not as Simple as It Seems: Underestimating the Positive Impact of Our Compliments on Others. *Personality and Social Psychology Bulletin* 2020; 47: 826-840. DOI: 10.1177/0146167220949003.

ABOUT THE AUTHORS

Damilola and Ifechukwude Adingupu have been together as a couple for 20 years, with 12 years of marriage experience. They are certified marriage mentors and marriage coaches, with formal education from Professional Christian Coaching Institute (https://professionalchristiancoaching.com/).

As a scientist, Dr. Damilola Adingupu has over 10 years of experience conducting research and performing literature reviews, so she is skilled in reviewing the research on marriages and relationships and putting together those resources for Thriving Relationships. Ifechukwude is a natural mentor who has the heart to share his experiences and life stories to impact other people's lives positively. Together they run their non-profit organization, TheMarriageAdvocates Canada (www.themarriageadvocates.ca) and run a marriage and relationship coaching practice.